THE ART O SUCCESSFUL BRAND COLLABORATIONS

PARTNERSHIPS WITH ARTISTS, DESIGNERS, MUSEUMS, TERRITORIES, SPORTS, CELEBRITIES, SCIENCE, GOOD CAUSES ... AND MORE

Géraldine Michel and Reine Willing

Routledge
Taylor & Francis Group

LONDON AND NEW YORK

First published 2020
by Routledge
2 Park Square, Milton Park, Abingdon, Oxon OX14 4RN

and by Routledge
52 Vanderbilt Avenue, New York, NY 10017

Routledge is an imprint of the Taylor & Francis Group, an informa business

© 2020 Géraldine Michel and Reine Willing

The right of Géraldine Michel and Reine Willing to be identified as authors of this work has been asserted by them in accordance with sections 77 and 78 of the Copyright, Designs and Patents Act 1988.

All rights reserved. No part of this book may be reprinted or reproduced or utilised in any form or by any electronic, mechanical, or other means, now known or hereafter invented, including photocopying and recording, or in any information storage or retrieval system, without permission in writing from the publishers.

Trademark notice: Product or corporate names may be trademarks or registered trademarks, and are used only for identification and explanation without intent to infringe.

British Library Cataloguing-in-Publication Data
A catalogue record for this book is available from the British Library

Library of Congress Cataloging-in-Publication Data
Names: Michel, Géraldine, author. | Willing, Reine, author.
Title: The art of successful brand collaborations: partnerships with artists, designers, museums, territories, sports, celebrities, science, good causes…and more / Géraldine Michel and Reine Willing.
Description: Milton Park, Abingdon, Oxon; New York, NY: Routledge, 2020. | Includes bibliographical references and index.
Identifiers: LCCN 2019036566 (print) | LCCN 2019036567 (ebook) | ISBN 9781138499607 (hardback) | ISBN 9781138499614 (paperback) | ISBN 9781351014472 (ebook)
Subjects: LCSH: Strategic alliances (Business)—Management. | Joint ventures—Management. | Branding (Marketing)
Classification: LCC HD69.S8 M525 2020 (print) | LCC HD69.S8 (ebook) | DDC 658.8/27—dc23
LC record available at https://lccn.loc.gov/2019036566
LC ebook record available at https://lccn.loc.gov/2019036567

ISBN: 978-1-138-49960-7 (hbk)
ISBN: 978-1-138-49961-4 (pbk)
ISBN: 978-1-351-01447-2 (ebk)

Typeset in Minion Pro
by codeMantra

THE ART OF SUCCESSFUL BRAND COLLABORATIONS

Brand collaborations are widely considered the art of the perfect match. This book is a guide to understanding the process of brand collaborations and explains the key factors of success to build specific forms of collaborations between divers partners. *The Art of Successful Brand Collaborations* gives tangible examples of partnerships between various kinds of internationally renowned artists, celebrities, brands and companies such as Coca-Cola, Louis Vuitton, Unicef, MoMA, David Beckham, Pharrell Williams and Van Gogh.

In this vivid study, the academic and practitioner author team outline deep knowledge about the advantages and economic benefits of this marketing strategy. This includes additional meaning, improvement of the brand image, attracting new customers within different target groups and the development of the brand in new markets.

Filled with interviews from practitioners and vital academic and professional insights, this book is an essential guide for brand managers, professors and students to better understand and successfully implement the process of brand collaborations.

Géraldine Michel is Professor in Marketing at the Sorbonne Business School, University Paris 1 Panthéon-Sorbonne in France where she is Director of the Chair "Brands & Values" and Director of the research laboratory. She studies particularly the role of brands for consumers and employees based on social psychology. She is the author of four books on brand management and she has published in several academic journals. She lectures worldwide in countries such as France, China and Vietnam, and she has consulting engagements with companies on issues of brand development.

Reine Willing is the founder and CEO of 19 Mars, a global but niche consulting agency specializing in creating high quality partnerships between major brands and artists, celebrities, NGOs, good causes and foundations, alongside handling co-branding requests for limited editions, capsule collections and licensing deals. Based in Paris, she is highly involved in brand activism through partnerships and good cause marketing. An alumni of the Sorbonne University's Marketing Masters programme, she is currently also educating others about brand partnerships through lectures in various universities.

CONTENTS

CONTENTS

ACKNOWLEDGEMENTS

Writing this book was an accomplishment made possible thanks to many people – a real partnership! As co-authors, we would like to thank all the people who generously gave their time in accepting long interviews with us, and who talked candidly about the values and personal experiences of their brand partnerships. These include David Bloch (WWF International), Gianfranco Brunetti (LIDL), Chay Costello (MoMA), Ludovic du Plessis (Louis XIII), Paloma Escudero (UNICEF), Hugues Fabre (DS cars), Laurent Fiévet (Lab' Bel, BEL Group), Carlos Flemming (WME), Adam Petrick (PUMA), Press office of LuisaViaRoma, Isabel Salas Mendez (Peugeot), Sébastien Servaire (Servaire & Co), the fashion designer Kenzo Takada, Margareta Van Den Bosh (H&M) and Cheryl Vitali (Kiehl's). Without them, this book would have been far less inspirational and true to its message.

We'd also like to thank the companies who gave us the rights to the pictures in this book, including: Airbnb, Amazon, Ambush, Bel, Bic, Bmw, Chopard, Dior, DS, Estée Lauder, Evian, Kusmi-tea, Grand Palais, H&M, Häagendazs, Wimbledon, Heineken, Lego, Kenzo, Khiel's, Lacoste, Le bon marché, Lidl, Louis Vuitton, Louis XIII, LouisaViaRoma, Milka, Moulin Rouge, Nike, Nivea, L'Occitane, Pierre Hermé, Peugeot, Philips, PSG, Redbull, Roland Garros, Go-pro, Servaire, Swarovski, Vans, Musée Van Gogh, Veja, Ville de Paris, WWF and Zadig et Voltaire.

We'd both like to thank our collaborators at Agency 19-03, which includes Aurelia Thietart, who was a constant source of support and endless research during this process, and Jacqueline Holmes, who read, edited, and added to early drafts of the book. Our gratitude, for their kind help and dedication, goes to Jenny Ramaromisa, Nzinga Dixon, Clemence Chiquet, Camille Gianni, Julia de Man, Marine Lecroart, Mia Ferrari Mathis, Alice van der Aal and Eric Mathis.

We'd both like to thank all our colleagues and the students from the Sorbonne Business School (IAE Paris). We thank Samuel Haddad, Guizlane Kasmi, Alexandre Nassar and Valérie Zeitoun for reading the manuscript before the publication and for their input in the book. We would like to thank Jolhane Leite and Christian Menez for their original and rich examples. We are, in particular, grateful to Alexandre Nassar who collected and transcribed the consumer testimonies. Also, we give full acknowledgements to the marketing students at the Sorbonne Business School and the members of the Chair Brands & Values with whom we shared numerous conversations about brand collaborations and who give us inspirational contributions.

We must acknowledge our publisher Routledge for their confidence, support, and patience in this new and exciting project – we couldn't have done it without you! The amazing book cover design is due to the creative work and dedication of the global design agency Servaire & Co., Sebastien Servaire, Anne Pillard, and Amelie Anthome – a true pleasure to work with!

Introduction

In the quest for innovation and the search for new relationships with consumers, companies are moving into brand collaborations and long-term or short-term partnerships for an ephemeral collection and different forms of brand collaboration are increasing. The union strengthens both partners, so 1 + 1 > 2, and nothing seems to be stopping this interest in joining together brands, creators, artists, celebrities, NGOs, cultural institutions and territories, etc.

Until now, the term "co-branding" has often been associated with the launch of new products, or limited edition collections, launched in the world of fashion (H&M & Balmain, Adidas Stella McCartney) or cars (BMW & Louis Vuitton). Brand partnerships today are multiform – they can be envisaged with a variety of partners (brands, artists, territories, museums, etc.) and generate different kinds of creations (product, communication, events, experience, etc.). In this book we want to go beyond the idea of co-branding and show that, today, brand collaboration is a strategy that goes beyond the product and can give meaning to employees, consumers and citizens, involving both collaborations with retailers, NGOs, territories and also collaborations with celebrities that are associated with values or even social causes. In this sense, Nike's partnership with Colin Kaepernick, an American football player excluded from the National Football League and criticized by Donald Trump, is emblematic of a brand collaboration which goes beyond the co-branded product and that enters the social and political spheres.

In this book, taking into account the evolution of companies' practices, we consider brand collaborations as any type of partnership between a brand and a partner, aimed at a specific target. Like any union, with or without predecessors, brand collaborations can give birth to a new product but can also, rather than launching a new product, create a new event, a unique experience, a common advertising campaign, or may represent a sharing of the distribution network, etc. There are many types of partnerships; the difference between brand collaborations, and the classic "customer-supplier" or "joint-venture" partnerships, lies in the communication action set up, internally or externally, by the brands and their partners to show the interest in, and the uniqueness of, the collaboration. What we do together we could never have created if we had stayed alone. Brand collaboration is the art of partnership and the creation of something new. Knowing how to collaborate, combine, and enrich oneself with other worlds reflects a certain openness, a dynamism, a renewal that is positively valued by society today.

WHY HAVE WE WRITTEN THIS BOOK?

Given the extended role of brand collaborations and the increasingly strategic function of partnership departments in most companies, several questions emerge: What is the added value of a brand collaboration for consumers and clients? What are the benefits and risks of brand collaborations? Are they win-win situations or do they bring more benefits to one of the partners? To address these questions, it is important to consider the place of brand collaborations at the heart of brand management. Building a strong brand means building a brand that makes sense to both employees and consumers.[1] How do brand collaborations influence this construction of brand identity? To answer this question, this book is born from the pedagogical desire to better

---

1 Michel, G. (2017). *Au Coeur de la Marque, les Clés du Management de la Marque*, 3rd edition. Malakoff: Dunod.

understand brand collaboration strategies and from the idea of making the essential tools for its implementation accessible. Our goal is to show that brand collaborations go beyond partnerships to produce a new product or to develop a new advertising campaign for a limited period – brand collaboration represents a new philosophy for companies and brand management. Brand collaborations draw a new space of freedom where everything is made possible for brands with a "let's go spirit." Brand collaboration is also about successes, difficulties, problems, and failures. We have written this book to allow companies to share their experiences. Their stories, the backgrounds of their brand collaborations, provide an authentic picture for the readers. Finally, this book is also an encounter between the CEO of a renowned partnership agency and an acclaimed Professor of Marketing, both passionate about brand collaborations. Their partnership is perfectly encapsulated in this book.

WHO IS THIS BOOK FOR?

This book is dedicated to multiple targets: companies, students, and a wider audience.

For managers, this book provides a complete view of brand collaboration strategies. Because brand collaborations are growing in many companies and in different industries, and because little is known about its strategy, it is important to provide an in-depth vision to help companies and all types of organizations in the art of partnerships. This book provides companies with a multifaceted approach to brand collaboration that will enable them to set up relevant brand collaborations, developing their brands. By the end of this book, brand managers will be able to understand how brand collaborations create value for not just for the consumer, but also the company, and they will master the key strategies necessary to succeed. In particular, the last chapter will become an operational guide for all professionals wishing to set up a brand collaboration.

For students, this book provides a complete and accessible vision of brand collaboration strategies. Students will find in this book practical and original knowledge to better understand why and how to carry out brand collaborations, integrated into strategic brand management. Students will find many examples, in a wide variety of sectors, allowing them to assimilate this new knowledge as much as possible.

For a wider audience, this book is very accessible. It allows consumers to understand how brand collaborations are implemented by brands. Consumers' and managers' testimonials unveil the background to the brand collaborations proliferating on supermarket shelves, in department stores, in the industry, and throughout the service sector. Illustrated with more than 60 images, this book allows readers to discover, or rediscover, particular brand collaborations. It can be easily read, following the images and the managers' and consumers' testimonies.

HOW IS THIS BOOK ORGANIZED?

In order to have a better understanding of brand collaboration, this book follows a managerial approach. Highlighting current and new knowledge about brand collaborations, the two parts capture the essence and the main levers of this strategy and show how to define brand collaboration. In order to present original knowledge about brand collaboration, this book is based on three main principles:

- New knowledge diffusion: Presenting an original approach to brand collaboration.
- Pedagogy: Developing a co-branding guide for managers.
- Diversity: Analyzing brands in different sectors; for example, Business to Consumer or Business to Business.

This book, organized in two parts, shares a new vision of brand collaboration.

Part I, "A complete view of brand collaboration," focuses on presenting the different possible partners in brand collaborations and identifies the different creations made possible by the marriage between brands and these different partners. This first part is organized around seven chapters highlighting different kinds of collaborations and integrating testimonies from top managers in different industries. The 16 interviews unveil the background to various brand collaborations and tell unique stories about successful and less successful encounters. These testimonies help identify new trends in brand collaborations – more focused on co-construction and suggesting a 360° management of brand collaboration. Supported by multiple examples and consumer stories, this part shows how brand collaboration creates values internally and externally and reveals that beyond the launching of new products, brand collaborations also create unique experiences and emotional energy, and enlarge the commitment of brands in social and environmental concerns.

Part II, "Key strategies and methods for successful brand collaborations," presents the fundamental tools of brand management, such as brand identity, brand image, and the brand's legitimacy principle. A good knowledge of these tools is essential to carry out a brand collaboration. In a second step, this part shows that beyond the usual levers of a brand collaboration – organized around the notions of consistency, complementarity, unexpected marriage and added value for consumers – brand collaborations need new keys to succeed. Indeed, if a brand collaboration is at the heart of the brand management, it needs to take into account new specific levers (from product to values, from short-term to long-term, from storytelling to story-doing, etc.) to ensure a successful marriage and also to create value for both partners and consumers. This last part also contains an implementation guide, presenting the different steps essential to the realization of a brand collaboration. Starting with the choice of the partner and signature of the contract, through the negotiation between the partners and ending with the analysis of the brand collaboration's impact, this part will become the reference guide for all professionals who plan to start a brand collaboration.

Happy reading!!!

Géraldine Michel

Professor, Sorbonne Business School, Universtity Paris 1 Panthéon-Sorbonne, Director of the Chair "Brands & Values." Paris, France.

and Reine Willing

Founder, Agency 19-03, specialized in Partnerships, Co-brandings, Celebrity Endorsements, Limited Editions, Sponsorships, Good Cause and Brand Activism collaborations, based Paris, France and Miami, USA.

Image 1 *Géraldine Michel and Reine Willing*

PART I

A complete view of brand collaboration

Today, brand collaborations take many different forms. They represent a new Eldorado for brands looking for innovation, renewal, more visibility, and attractiveness. In this first part, we will analyze the practices of brand collaboration, identifying the different partners and forms of collaboration. This will be very helpful for managers wanting to know who they can engage in a partnership with and what they can develop together.

CHAPTER 1

Collaborations between consumer goods brands

When managers decide to associate two brands for defining a brand collaboration, they can install six different kinds of partnership depending on what they want to create (see Table 1.1): a co-branded product, a co-branded communication, a cross-sales promotion, a co-branded experience, a co-branded distribution and a brand collaboration dedicated to employees.

Table 1.1 Collaborations between consumer goods brands

Kinds of collaboration	Definition	Examples
Co-branded products (co-branding)	Collaboration between two brands involving the co-creation and co-naming of a new product	- Apple & Hermès - Huawei & Leica - Louis Vuitton & Supreme - Uniqlo & Disney
Co-branded communications	Collaboration between two brands involving the co-creation of a communication message	- Google & Oreo
Cross-sales promotions	Collaboration between two brands involving the creation of a common sales promotion	- Mc Donald's & Dragon Ball - Burger King & Barbie - BlablaCar & Total

(Continued)

Kinds of collaboration	Definition	Examples
Co-branded experiences	Collaboration between two brands involving the creation of a common experience, including events, common stores etc.	- Pierre Hermé & L'Occitane - Citadium & Instagram
Co-branded distribution	Collaboration between a retailer and a brand resulting, for the retailer, in exclusive distribution of the partner's products	- McDonald's & Coca-Cola - Quick & Pepsi - Starbucks & One water
Brand collaborations dedicated to employees	Collaboration between two companies involving a new product or service targeting employees	- DS & VanCleef and Arpel - DS & the Richemont creative academy - Air France & Christian Lacroix

1.1 WHEN CONSUMER GOODS BRANDS CREATE CO-BRANDED PRODUCTS TOGETHER

Among the different kinds of brand collaboration, the co-branding strategy is a collaboration between two or more brands based on the co-creation and co-naming of a new product. Both brands are thus visible on the co-branded product. This strategy involves the distinction between the "host brand" and the "guest brand." For instance, in the co-branding between Philips and Nivea, the "host brand" was Philips since the brand already existed on the razor market at the launch of

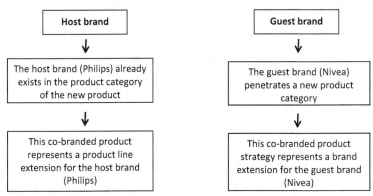

Figure 1.1 *The difference between host and guest brands*

the co-branded razor. Nivea would then be the guest brand adding the cream to the electric razor. Philips and Nivea collaborated in order to launch a new product enlarging the target of the host brand Philips and extending the territory of the guest brand Nivea in the men's shaving market.

The co-branded product strategy can take two main forms: either 1) the guest brand brings a tangible element related to its know-how, or 2) the guest brand transmits only its symbolic elements (Cegarra and Michel, 2001).

1) THE CO-BRANDED PRODUCT INCLUDES A TANGIBLE ELEMENT FROM THE GUEST BRAND

The co-branded product with a tangible element from the guest brand is based on the integration of an element from the guest brand into the new co-branded product, involving product innovation. In the food market, we can cite the example of Evian and Kusmi tea. Both brands collaborated to launch a new tea-based drink. The complementarity of ingredients brings an added value to consumers looking for new tastes.

Image 1.1 *A new based-tea drink by Evian and Kusmi Tea*

In the household market, the collaboration between Huawei and Leica (a German brand of cameras and optics) allows consumers to make better pictures with their mobile phone. The Huawei P9 phones uses dual cameras – a 12-megapixel color and one – a 12-megapixel colour camera alongside a 12-megapixel black and white lens – which captures 200% more light and let owners refocus their photos after they have been taken. This innovation, the result of a collaboration between the Chinese tech firm and German camera-maker Leica, can help Huawei promote itself as a premium brand and expand its market share.

Within the strategy of co-branded products, the guest brand can be a business to business brand (B2B); in other words, the guest brand can be an ingredient brand such as Intel, Gore-Tex or Teflon (Gore-Tex and Teflon waterproof membrane brands). Consumers have become more sensitive to ingredient brands that provide an additional product benefit and are seen as a pledge for real differentiation (Moon and Sprott, 2016). For instance, based on their expertise in crystal-stone manufacture and shaping, the

Image 1.2 *Swarovski* & *Moulin Rouge*

Swarovski brand has developed numerous partnerships in different sectors and with multiple brands. For instance, they design crystal components both for BMW cars and for Moët & Chandon champagne. When Swarovski's customers want to communicate with their consumers,or want to bring added value to their products, Swarovksi might suggest the label "Crystals from Swarovski," depending on the positioning and the distribution of the crystal products. This label is even more appropriate when Swarovski designs specific stones to meet the requirements of its partners. For instance, in the world of entertainment, Swarovski worked with Moulin Rouge (a Parisian cabaret) – the show *Féérie* highlights the best craftsmanship using the premium material of Swarovski crystals. The revue includes 60 dancers wearing over 1,000 costumes and 800 custom-made pairs of shoes, all embellished with thousands of sparkling Swarovski crystals. To celebrate the union between Swarovski and Moulin

Rouge, a film was produced to provide an exclusive peek behind the curtain, revealing the extraordinary level of creativity that goes into co-producing the show.

Beyond the manufacture of crystals for its customers and branding partners, Swarovski can provide knowledge about the job of stone shaping and can share its brand content to help their customers promote their final products. For instance, the relationship between Swarovski and Zadig & Voltaire (a French premium fashion brand) allowed to embellish the jeans of the fashion brand. In addition Zadig & Voltaire enjoyed the training provided by Swarovski explaining how to showcase their limited collection

Image 1.3 *Swaroski & Zadig & Voltaire*

of jeans. This kind of partnership shows that Swarovski, concerned to maintain the collaboration as long as possible, knows how to promote loyalty in their clients.

Specific examples of ingredient brands from the Business to Business model, engaging in collaborations with competitor brands, show unbalanced benefits between the partner brands (Desai and Keller, 2002). Overall, ingredient brands gain more advantage from the co-branding strategy than host brands. An ingredient brand, such as Intel, teams up with brands such as Compaq, Sony and Toshiba. These computer brands can claim strong product performances and can take advantage of a famous Intel ingredient component. However, these collaborations do not allow a strong differentiation for the host brand as the ingredient brand Intel is associated with all its competitors.

2) THE CO-BRANDED PRODUCT BASED ON THE SYMBOLIC ELEMENT OF THE GUEST BRAND

The co-branded product without a tangible element from the guest brand represents a collaboration where the guest brand does not bring tangible ingredients or components to define the co-branded product but transmits its symbolic image, its symbolic universe. This strategy is frequently used in the car market because the symbolic dimension of the guest brand allows enlarging the target of car constructors (Michel, 2017). The alliance between Fiat 500 and Gucci enabled the car manufacturer to claim a luxury positioning, referring to the Italian fashion industry. This important success provided Gucci with a "sportswear" positioning. In the same vein, Fiat 500 collaborated with Guerlain. This is again a success for Fiat as it presented the new car as an accessory for the fashionistas. In this automotive market, where consumers are more and more demanding and where it is more and more difficult to attract buyers, the co-branded product promotes sales.

as BMW Art Car

EXAMPLES: THE CO-BRANDED PRODUCT IN THE CAR INDUSTRY

Supposed to nourish the image of each of the brands and animate the communication around the product, co-branded products in the automotive sector connect more and more diverse companies. We can mention the BMW and Louis Vuitton collaborations, Ferrari and Apple, and Mercedes and Swarovski as car manufacturers take advantage of the expertise of their partners. BMW includes Louis Vuitton luggage made especially for its car; Ferrari integrates the high-tech devices of Apple; and Mercedes uses Swarovski crystals in its board tables. These different partnerships seek to show that the vehicle is aimed at a certain segment of customers. The Peugeot 106, Roland Garros, chic and sporty, applies the color of red clay to different elements of the car and tries to attract a sporting customer. On the other hand, Lolita Lempicka-Nissan Micra, with a chic and feminine touch, strives to reach urban women. For the guest brand, this collaboration is a way to become known by a wider audience and to enable them to discover its identity. Similarly, Leica, the brand of high-end cameras, by co-signing with the Saab 9-3 model, offering a Leica C11 APS, has sought to make itself known to a wider audience. Although partnerships serve different purposes, it must be remembered that the success of such collaborations lies in the added value of the co-branded product to consumers.

In the food market, the co-branded product strategy without an intangible element from the guest brand is related to the symbolic co-branded product where the guest brand brings all its creativity. The Coca light bottles, with the flashy colors of the brand Sonia Rykiel (a French designer brand), emphasize the happy and elegant dimensions of the soda in order to attract a female customer. When San Pellegrino collaborates with the jeweler Bvlgari to provide a bottle a limited collection, it is to tell a new story about the Italian

Image 1.4 *Veja & Deyrolle*

cultural background of the water brand. San Pellegrino, sharing common values with Bvlgari around elegance and Italian excellence, can highlight its premium positioning with this partnership.

Co-branded products are more and more numerous also in the fashion industry. The Japanese designer and his brand Yamamoto have been providing, for more than ten years, a limited shoes and clothes collection called Y3 with the Adidas logo allowing the successful marriage between sport and the Japanese style. Veja, the eco-responsible sneakers brand, has teamed up with Deyrolle, one of the best known companies of entomology and taxidermy, whose vocation is to show the beauty of Nature, by launching a limited collection of shoes and clothes. The co-branded products are distinguished by the drawings of pedagogical charts of insects, and especially the charts of butterflies. This choice is important in making the link between both brands and highlighting their environmental concerns. This partnership tells a seductive story for consumers about the silk of the butterfly and the silk used in Veja sneakers.

EXAMPLE: SUPERHEROES AND CO-BRANDED PRODUCTS

Marvel is the leading company in the entertainment industry that produces superhero movies (Captain America, Hulk, Iron Man, Namor, Batman, etc.). To exploit all the benefits that its characters can offer, Marvel licenses its superheroes with co-branded products such as toys, school supplies, clothing, and even perfume. Licensing plays a key role in Marvel's turnover and it also maximizes the global exposure of its brands in a short amount of time. Marvel has built up strategic relationships with successful brands such as Lego, Samsung, Coca-Cola, MasterCard, Hasbro (American toys and games brand), Reebok, Absolut Vodka and many others. A study analyzed the effects of superheroes co-branding according to the concept of the partner brands (Hégner and Peixoto, 2017). They make distinctions between functional and expressive brand concepts, which are based on two different classifications of consumer needs. Functional brands solve functional needs (e.g. Michelin, Lenovo), while expressive brands solve expressive needs, which can be internally generated desires, such as self-enhancement, status, etc. (e.g. Audi, Apple). Their survey concludes that forming a brand alliance with a superhero character is a good strategy to follow, particularly for brands with an expressive brand concept. These brands should aim to identify a superhero character that can pose a high perceived fit for consumers looking for symbolic products. For functional brands, the fit between the partners' brands seems to be less important. The good evaluation of co-branding with low-fit alliances between a functional brand and the superhero are quite unexpected and interesting revelations. Thus, the key takeaway of this study is that both perceived fit and brand concept are important factors when forming a brand alliance with a superhero character (Hégner and Peixoto, 2017). Therefore, one should consider both of these variables before making a licensing agreement with a company owning a superhero character, in order to increase brand equity.

Functional vs Exessive brands.
brand partnership → Symbolic products)

In the fashion industry, the partnership between retailers' brands and fashion brands are numerous: H&M, Uniqlo and Weekday are three retailers excelling in the art of collaboration, but each one follows different strategies. H&M gives huge media exposure to its collaborations with Balmain or Kenzo causing endless queues at the launch of its capsule collections. Its ephemeral partnerships create value for the customer in search of affordable luxury items. As for Uniqlo, the brand opts for discreet and durable partnerships. The long-term Uniqlo & Christophe Lemaire (a French ready-to-wear stylist) collaboration focuses on simple, comfortable and portable clothing in a multitude of ways. Like Christophe Lemaire, Ines de la Fressange (a French fashion designer), through her own brand, has been collaborating with the Japanese brand since 2014. The aim of these different collaborations is to draw inspiration from universes that Uniqlo does not occupy and does not wish to emulate. The collaborations between brands and retailers are opportunities for the exclusive brands to be accessible for a short period, limiting brand dilution (Nabec, Pras and Laurent, 2016).

There is an increase in brand alliances in higher education. Indeed, schools collaborate with different partners to complement or provide new programmes. For instance, the European Business School INSEAD collaborates with Warthon University (University of Pennsylvania) and Kellog School of Management (NorthWestern University) to provide student exchanges for their MBA students. Also, the departments of Art History and Archeology at Columbia University and at Paris 1 Panthéon-Sorbonne University offer a double degree in Master. This dual degree offers students the unique opportunity to study in two of the world's best training courses in the field. Indeed, students appreciate the double degrees and they evaluate them positively in terms of the brand image of their partners, their complementarity and, most importantly, regarding the added value of the dual degree (Naidoo and Hollebeek, 2016). Indeed, today it has been shown that dual degrees, in collaboration with similarly ranked universities, are unlikely to generate added value compared to single degrees irrespective of the value proposition. In conclusion, schools' collaborations have to highlight a strong and specific complementarity to attract students (Kalafatis et al., 2016).

In the cosmetic sector, the Japanese cosmetic brand, Face Shop, collaborates with Coca-Cola in order to launch five products for their Asian make-up market. The products assert the colors of the famous drink brand including a special lipstick in five shades with the smell of Coca-Cola soda. All products are packaged in the fizzy cola's eye-catching signature red and white.

In another register, brands can collaborate by providing a new service with a high added value for the consumers: e.g. Uber. The right song can turn a stressful morning into a peaceful commute, which is why Uber launched a partnership with Pandora and Spotify Premium – two ways to customize the client's ride allowing them to play music from their Uber app. This partnership creates great added value for consumers. However, the marriage with Uber is not easy for their partners, who fear they will be impacted by the negative buzz generated by the American taxi operator. When the criticism of Uber arose, its partner Spotify decided to continue the partnership but without any press campaign. The constant debate, raised by this story, is the evaluation of the risk to be impacted by the negative buzz about its partner and the decision to stop or continue the collaboration to preserve its reputation. There is no simple answer. It is important to remember that the most important thing is to ensure consistency with brand values.

Whether collaborations are short-lived or long-lasting, host brands are mainly looking for sources of inspiration to create new emotions among their customers while guest brands are looking for more visibility among a wider, new audience.

CONSUMER TESTIMONY

Alexandre, 24-years-old, single, student, French, Vans & several partners (interviewed in October 2018)

I always liked the Vans brand. It gives off values of youth, energy, very urban style and a little offbeat. At 18, I was mainly interested in their co-branded collections, especially with Disney and

Peanuts, universes that fascinate me. I bought all their co-branded backpacks, the Vans bags with the logo written in large but on a print of 101 Dalmatians or Snoopy; and, in general, only 40€.

My arrival in the world of work changed these dress habits a little. Although tolerated in the office, it is impossible to appear in front of a customer or event with such an accessory... Almost a year ago, I received an email from Vans that changed the situation – a collaboration between Vans and Karl Lagerfeld. In this collection, a perfect backpack: black, leather, an original side with a quilted but extreme sobriety for the brand. Of course, such an accessory cost me 300€. I think Vans understood its audience well. Teenage targets have reached adulthood and are moving away from the brand. This co-branding allowed them to create a more upscale limited collection for young active adults. The sobriety of the products and their high price suggest that the target was not the teenage skater with ripped jeans...

This strategy is confirmed with a capsule collection this year in collaboration with the Van Gogh Museum (see Chapter 3). Are we addressing a more mature population when we offer articles inspired by pictorial art?

1.2 WHEN CONSUMER GOODS BRANDS CLAIM A COMMON MESSAGE TOGETHER

Co-branded communication is the collaboration between brands to develop a common communication campaign. It is characterized by the association of two or more brands on a communication medium, of any nature whatsoever (poster, press announcement, TV spot, video, Instagram...), excluding packaging or tangible products. The main purpose of the co-branded communication is to get the attention of consumers. For instance, the Opel brand communication campaign associated with the Durex brand ("For a pleasure with maximum safety, Durex recommends Opel Corsa") has allowed the car brand to claim a safety value.

In another context, Google and Oreo (a commercial brand from Mendelez International) have established a communication partnership without financial exchange but where the two parties have a lot to gain. The collaboration comes down to the use of the name Oreo to name Google Android 8.0 and, in exchange, a vast free communication campaign for the brand Oreo. The different names of Android versions have always a name inspired by a biscuit. In 2013, Google chose the Kitkat brand for its Android 4.4; in 2018 it is therefore Oreo. What are the benefits of such a partnership? For Google as for Oreo, the interest is to strengthen the reputation of their respective brands and communicate massively around them. The mascot of Android 8.0 is a superhero with a cape and shield (cookie-shaped), a dream character to communicate on social networks and to advertise Oreos. In addition, the Oreo logo will appear on smartphones when the device is turned on. The biscuit brand is thus integrated into an object that is used repetitively, daily. Finally, associating its name with Google – even if the web giant is regularly criticized – gives Oreo the image of an up-to-date, modern brand. If, through Google, Oreo appears more modern, the logic for Google is significantly different. Indeed, thanks to these treats – and especially via social networks – it can reach an audience that is not necessarily familiar with new technologies.

In the car industry, since 1970, the brand Renault has shown its collaboration with the brand Elf (a French brand of engine lubricant) in the slogan "Renault recommends Elf" on cars and in advertising booklets. Nissan also collaborates with the Stonyfield Farm in France to promote their electric cars. They communicate about this partnership and the co-branded advertising highlights the daring match between organic products and electric cars.

To make an impression, Burger King and Gillette have not hesitated to join forces with the Movember Foundation, which wishes to make men aware of the health problems that affect them; they die on average six years before women because of the lack of cancer prevention. The idea of this advertising campaign is to create awareness of men's health by encouraging men to grow a mustache. During one month, Burger King fans are invited to post photographs of their mustaches on social media (#Kingstachechallenge) and Movember will use images generated as part of its charitable fundraising. On the first of November the participants receive a free razor from Gillette to shave off their beards. This brand collaboration allows Burger King to engage in societal topics. For its part, Gillette values its razors for a close shave and the Movember Foundation benefits from a humorous communication relay.

1.3 WHEN CONSUMER GOODS BRANDS PROVIDE CROSS-SALES PROMOTIONS TOGETHER

The cross-sales promotion involves the collaboration between both brands in order to define a common sales promotion. Buying a product, the consumer takes an advantage of the partner brand. Perhaps the most visible cross-promotional campaign involves McDonald's Happy Meals and the movie *Star Trek: The Motion Picture*. The restaurant has teamed up with Hollywood studios and toy manufacturers who want to tout their latest wares via kids' meals. Little girls at Burger King Restaurants are offered Barbie dolls when they buy a kid's menu. Credit cards associated with car manufacturers (Visa/Peugeot) or airlines (American Express/Air France) can accumulate points either to benefit from a reduction in the after-sales service of Peugeot or to increase its number of "Miles" that can be used later when purchasing Air France tickets. In the field of video games, the purchase of a Google Play card has earned the players of Clash Royale 12€ of gems, the currency of the virtual war game. There are many more examples: the Nesquick brand has offered its consumers a Cars brand video game with the purchase of a Nesquick cereal pack. Cross-sales promotion between two or more brands can create a form of relationship between brands. In the transport sector, the Total brand supports carpooling in partnership with BlaBlaCar and offers a fuel card or a washing card to drivers for their first journey. On the website of Total you can see on a full page "15€ * fuel or 40€ * wash offered for your first trip via BlaBlaCar!" Coupling a co-branded product and cross-sales promotion, Uniqlo and McDonald's have now teamed up to celebrate the Big Mac's 50th anniversary. The capsule collection offers graphic T-shirts in the iconic red and yellow colors. With each piece emblazoned with eye-catching graphics, showing the Big Mac's milestone achievement, Japanese customers receive a Big Mac coupon upon purchase.

In the hospitality context, Airbnb and Lego (Danish plastic construction toys) collaborated to organize a game contest offering one night in the Lego house. In order to win this magic night, people had to describe their dream Lego construction with an unlimited number of Lego bricks. This partnership allows Airbnb to provide a magic experience to its clients and Lego demonstrates again its capacity to develop the imagination of adults and children.

These cross-sales promotions, generating specific advantages, create a real added value for consumers who are more and more demanding and increasingly bombarded with advertising.

Image 1.5 *Airbnb & Lego*

1.4 WHEN CONSUMER GOODS BRANDS ORGANIZE EVENTS TOGETHER

Brand collaborations can involve the creation of new events, such as ceremonies for product launchings, but also spectacular street marketing operations. These co-branded events are usually unusual or exceptional but the main objective is to promote the brand, product, or company to different audiences. For this, it is important to attract the attention of consumers and to surprise them. It is, therefore, essential to obtain significant media coverage of the event co-organized by the two partner brands. The advantage of brand collaborations in this type of experience is to be able to take advantage of the social network fanbases of both brands, which can potentially increase the total audience.

At the launch of Pierre Hermé and L'Occitane's 1000m^2 concept store on the Champs-Elysees, the experience was able to benefit from the social networks of both brands. The unprecedented marriage of the pastry chef with the cosmetics brand has been the stimulus to encourage the consumer

Image 1.6 *Pierre Hermé & L'Occitane store*

to discover the exclusive products of both brands and to assist in their manufacture.

This experience based on the co-branded store integrates at the same time co-branded products (for example, perfumes inspired by the pastry, and pastries inspired by the cosmetic universe) and co-branded experiences through a specific retail experience. The meeting between the worlds of gastronomy and cosmetics allows the two actors to reach a public in search of a "French-style" know-how, where the brands exchange signs of authenticity: culinary versus natural, gustatory versus olfactory, artisanal versus patrimonial. The collaboration between these two brands embodies a major trend in retail that consists of transforming stores into places of experience.

In the same vein of retail experience, Citadium collaborated with Instagram and four startups. Citadium, millennials' temple of pop culture, hosted an ephemeral corner shop highlighting four brands that grew thanks to Instagram. This brand collaboration put a distributor, a social network and four fashion and decoration brands around the table. It is a relatively complex operation where the legitimacy of each stakeholder must remain valid for the client.

Image 1.7 *Co-branded product Parfume L'Occitane & Pierre Hermé (Figuier Rose)*

On a larger scale, Le Bon Marché, a French premium retailer, invited nearly 130 brands as part of the "Let's Go Logo" operation. For Le Bon Marché, the 130 brands created exclusive capsule collections playing with their identities. The categories of products were introduced as ready-to-wear, accessories, home, beauty, or surprising everyday objects. The multiplicity and unexpectedness of the marriages between brands generated a huge buzz.

Image 1.8 *Le Bon Marché "Let's go Logo"*
(collaboration between a department store and several brands in the retail place)

The exhibition "Let's Go Logo!" offers brands a space of freedom to imagine offbeat products. This resulted in capsule collections never seen before with: Aalto, Bumble and Bumble, Carven, Céline, Chiara Ferragni, Christian Louboutin, Fendi, Guerlain, Isabel Marant, Jerôme Dreyfuss, Kiehl's, Kitsune, Koché, Loewe, Mira Mikati, Miu Miu, etc. Le Bon Marché used to work with artists, but this time, in order to create surprise, it encouraged unexpected products from their invited brands. In the same vein, the retailer Le Bon Marché collaborated with the famous sportswear brand Off White, creating an exhibition inspired by its white universe and offering a new capsule collection designed by its founder Virgil Abloh. For each collaboration, the objective of the luxury retailer Le Bon Marché is to create a unique experience for their clients, centred around creativity and exclusivity.

In another sector, Airbnb also relies on new partnerships to highlight the experience and their proximity to consumers. Sleeping in front of the Big Apple on Ellis Island, in Holmenkollen, or at the top of the Norwegian Olympic Ski Jumping Hill or in the heart of the Brazilian Maracana Stadium – so many places in which it is usually not possible to spend a night but where Airbnb has managed to establish a partnership.

As a last example, the Airbnb brand has partnered with the Aquarium of Paris to offer a night in a water room that aims to raise awareness of the disappearance of sharks and mitigate their terrible reputation.

Image 1.9 *Airbnb & Brazilian Macarana Stadium*

Image 1.10 *Airbnb & Aquarium of Paris*

Overall, the purpose of these collaborations is to bring new experiences to customers and arouse a strong curiosity around the brand. For Airbnb these collaborations with unusual partners are strong vectors of public relationship helping the acquisition of new customers on their site.

In Asia (Singapore), an interesting collaboration stimulated consumers' nostalgia. Tiffany & Co partnered with local bakery brand "Tiong Bahru Bakery" to make the first scene of the movie *Breakfast at Tiffany's* a reality. The jeweller set up a booth, outside of its store, providing free coffee and croissants. The marriage recreated the iconic Audrey Hepburn moment in the movie *Breakfast at Tiffany's* (1961) by having breakfast while peering into a Tiffany's boutique. Fifty-seven years later, visitors could post a picture of the coffee cart with hashtags such as #tiffanypaperflowers and #tiongbahrubakery

1.5 WHEN A RETAILER CONFERS EXCLUSIVE DISTRIBUTION TO A BRAND

Co-branded distribution means a collaboration between a retailer and a brand involving for the retailer an exclusive distribution of the brand partner. We can consider as brand collaboration where a retailer selects exclusive brands for its clients. When a client of Quick (a Belgian fast food restaurant chain) orders a Cola, she/he does not have the choice; they will be given a Pepsi Cola. This partnership demonstrates a differentiation from Mcdonald's which provides Coca-Cola in its restaurant. Similarly, Starbucks has extended its partnership with ethical water brand One Water into five new European countries. The deal means that bottled water in over 700 Starbucks' stores in France, Germany, Austria, Switzerland and the Netherlands will now be exclusively One Water. This collaboration shows Starbuck's support for the ethical One brand, committed it to several NGOs and used its profits to fund water projects in the world's poorest communities. A survey reveals that the choice of exclusive brands by retailers influences the intention of consumers to visit the stores (Arnett et al., 2010).

Among partnerships between retailers, we can mention the example of the collaboration between Shell and Burger King. On the roads in Morocco, Burger King is established in Shell service stations. This collaboration allows Shell to offer the best service to customers with as many comforts as possible and this allows Burger King to set up fast food restaurants faster in Morocco. It seems that some drivers change their itinerary to stop in a service station with a Burger King.

1.6 WHEN BRANDS COLLABORATE TO TARGET EMPLOYEES

When DS automotive company decided to train their employees in the culture of French luxury, they created their own school and they also decided to collaborate with two famous luxury brands. In the DS academy camp, the employees learn the know-how of the design and the work of the craftsmen cellars in order to integrate the brand history that they will share with the clients. Also, DS employees go to the school of Van Cleef and Arpel who initiate them into the refinement and the knowledge from a craft point of view. They also learn the sale methods of the luxury sector. In China, the collaboration is operated with Richemont academy. These collaborations allow DS employees to be embedded in the automotive culture but also mix in this French culture, taking the luxury codes from different sectors such as fashion and jewelry.

In another context, we can remember the collaboration in the 90s between Apple and Adidas targeting Apple employees. Indeed, Apple and Adidas made a partnership to manufacture a limited edition of sneakers with the Apple rainbow logo. They were first sold to lucky Apple employees and today these unique co-branded sneakers can be sold in auctions for up to $30,000.

TRANSCEND POTENTIAL MISCONCEPTIONS

- You can make a partnership with an unfamiliar brand if you ensure high fit between both brands.
- You can combine opposite brand's universes if the collaboration brings added value to consumers.
- If your partner gets bad press, before stopping the collaboration evaluate if the crisis questions your brand values.

INTERVIEW WITH MARGARETA VAN DEN BOSH
Creative Advisor at H&M

"Making luxury more affordable"

Keywords: trending gifts, mass vs. luxury

Actors: H&M, Iconic Fashion Designers

H&M is a Swedish multinational clothing-retail company founded in 1947, operating in 69 countries with over 4,500 stores. H&M is the second largest retailer in the clothing business just behind Zara and ahead of Gap Inc. as of 2018. The company has a significant online presence, with online shopping available in 44 markets. With collections for women, men, teenagers, children and babies, and decorations, the H&M product range also includes sportswear, underwear, cosmetics, accessories, and shoes. The range includes everything from sparkling gala outfits and exclusive designer collaborations to everyday basics and high-performance yoga wear to help fashion fans across the world dress their personal style.

In 2004, H&M's yearly designer collaborations started with Karl Lagerfeld, to be followed by collaborations with some of the world's biggest designers and fashion icons. Many top names have lined up to work with H&M, from red-carpet regulars such as Roberto Cavalli to avant-garde conceptualists Viktor & Rolf. The majority of these collections sell out in hours and hit the secondary market for two or three times the price of the originals. H&M also partners up with many celebrities: Beyoncé in 2013 for

Table 1.2 H&M fashion designer collaborations timeline

2004 Karl Lagerfeld	2012 Marni, Margiela
2005 Stella Mc Cartney	2013 Isabel Marant
2006 Viktor & Rolf	2014 Alexander Wang
2007 Roberto Cavalli	2015 Balmain
2008 Comme des Garçons	2016 Kenzo
2009 Matthew Williamson	2017 Erdem
2010 Jimmy Shoe	2018 Moschino
2011 Versace	2019 Giambattista Valli

swimsuits, taking a huge step into pop culture territory; David Beckham in 2012 for the bodywear collection, Nicky Minaj, Jessie Williams. H&M is furthermore supporting good causes through its foundation, such as UNICEF, to which H&M reverse a certain amount out of sales to support young children with disabilities or WWF.

1) How did the collaborations evolve over the past 14 years?

Since our first start in collaboration with Karl Lagerfeld in 2004, we have grown more professional through practice year after year – at the start, collaborations were quite chaotic in terms of logistic and internal organization. We still learn new things with each collaboration. Also, what has evolved since 2004 is how we engage the marketing and communication around the collaboration: there is much more announcement in advance, much more social media – with the bloggers and the influencers.

Despite our various collaborations, each collaboration serves to be a fresh start since every designer is unique and each one as has different ideas of doing, different wishes and different constraints. Every time we choose a new partner/fashion designer, it must be – first of all – someone that we like a lot, then it must be something very different from the previous collaboration, as well as someone that I feel that it is the right time for in the moment of fashion.

Throughout our different collaboration experiences, we have noticed customers love glamourous collections such as Versace, Balmain, which they fight for. Whereas the collection we made in partnership with "Comme des Garçons" was less successful and less sought after by our customers. When deciding which luxury brand house to collaborate with, we need to consider different aspects. We chose Alexander Wang because we had never made a sport collection and I think he really brought sport into fashion. He is a great designer and someone that I've been looking at for a while and he is the first American that we have collaborated with. Whereas with Olivier Rousteing (Balmain), we chose to collaborate with him as we were impressed by his work ethos: he works really closely with his team and is a team player, which hasn't always been the case as the designers we have worked with have all been very different personalities.

Olivier has a clear vision, but he also listens – he listens to advice and input and then he listens again, he's very easy to work with in that sense.

Our last collaboration was with Moschino and was launched on 8 November 2018. The campaign is said to be a "radically innovative TV concept enmeshing social and traditional media to create a multi-platform takeover – a captivating new "zapping" experience for the digital world."

2) What are H&M's expectations for each collaboration?

We do collaborations as a way of offering a gift to our customers. Thanks to collaborations, we demonstrate to the public how we can engage in many different things whilst still ensuring good quality and good prices.

The idea behind forming partnerships is to make luxury more affordable, but their inevitable buzz and slim production runs often result in frenzied scrums to purchase and vast mark-ups on eBay. The main objective for H&M is not to increase sales as it usually costs a lot of money to build a collaboration. We do it for PR purposes as well. When H&M collaborates with large luxury brands, the luxury brands themselves are benefiting from H&M's customers since it is a new audience of customers. When Jeremy Scott announced the new collaboration with H&M, he mentioned how excited he was about being able to connect through fashion to more fans, more than he has ever been able to. This collaboration would allow for him to share his work with larger crowds, as it would be sold at more affordable prices.

3) What did these partnerships bring to the fashion designers involved?

Elbaz is quoted as saying: "I didn't feel that I'm doing project that it is about a dress for less it was not Lanvin going out at a lower price but it was about H&M going out the luxury business." Consuelo Castiglioni, former designer at Marni said: "It's great to speak to a wider audience and in particular to a younger generation."

4) What are the fruits of each collaboration?

Throughout our years of expertise in collaborations, we have grown aware of our success when it comes to partnerships.

In 2004 with Karl Lagerfeld, when shops opened on 12 November, the collection sold out within minutes. In 2013, Isabel Marant had a 100% sell out rate and saw zero discounting. With the average sell through occurring within seven days, this collaboration, though not restocked, was a big success for H&M. It had an average price point 118% higher than H&M's mainline average price point and there was a 46% lift in number of products selling out that month, compared to November 2013. Our capsule collection in 2015 with Balmain benefited our brand as it brought us hype and publicity. Indeed, H&M stores around the world witnessed huge queues, with shoppers lining up 12 hours prior to the start of the collaboration sale. Similarly, hm.com was quickly overwhelmed with demand, showing many shoppers a message that read: "We have a lot of visitors on the site right now. This is due to the high level of interest in our latest collection."

Pieces from the collection quickly started to appear on eBay, with extortionate mark-ups. An embellished blazer that sold for £399.99 in store, sold for £3,300 on the auction site. That amount of money would easily get you a mainline Balmain jacket. The collaboration was heavily promoted, with H&M beginning to drip feed teasers from as early as May this year. Several high-profile models were involved – Gigi Hadid, Jourdan Dunn and Kendall Jenner – who have over 50 million Instagram followers between them, meaning exposure was especially high. I believe that collaborations are essential in order to ensure the success of a fashion brand – collaborations are a method to capture your consumers attention, and leave them excited and anxious for new products. The key is to think about the culture that inspires our young costumers: "celebrity culture, the art; movie and music world…. As a designer you must have your eyes, ears, everything open."

5) Who worked on this collaboration?

When we work with fashion designers such as Karl Lagerfeld, Elbaz, we don't need our team of designers. The fashion designer makes the sketches and then someone from H&M has to translate it for the production. In some cases, such as when working with like "Comme des Garçons" or "Lanvin" the fashion designer makes the patterns.

6) What were the most difficult parts of the partnership?

Keeping the collaboration secret while working with one of fashion's most prolific social media stars becomes a bigger challenge with each new launch – not least for the designer involved! Adapting to the fashion designers' expectations is one of the difficult parts of a partnership. For example, Karl Lagerfeld wanted to do a fashion show and Rei Kawakubo (from Comme des Garçons) doesn't want to do many interviews. Therefore, we could not have the same type of event we've done before. Sometimes we disagree but we always want to please fashion designers and make them happy.

7) What do you believe were the keys of success to this partnership?

Each fashion designer we've worked with was impressed by the good quality of the products we develop – this is the main key success of our collaborations. We have also a very good marketing team working on each collaboration and the whole together is becoming very successful – thanks to fantastic films (such as the one with Karl Lagerfeld who takes part in the production).

Image 1.11 *Black dress H&M & comme des garçons*

Image 1.12 *Store H&M & Comme des garçons*

LUISAVIAROMA

INTERVIEW WITH LUISAVIAROMA
Press Office

"Exclusivity is the new luxury: fast, unexpected, and extremely limited in types of product collaborations"

Keywords: exclusive in house, e-store only

Actors: LuisaViaRoma and partner brands

LuisaViaRoma is an Italian luxury retailer, created in 1930 by the parents of Andrea

Panconesi, Chief Executive of the brand) and has been an online store since 1999. Today, the e-store has 5 million visitors per month. LuisaViaRoma is now identified all over the world as a cutting-edge concept online store, aware of young talent and of the possibilities offered by new technologies. Today, the LVR e-shop is translated into nine languages and offers delivery in 200 countries. Since 2000, the company has ventured into philanthropy, art, and home furnishing with their latest project being Fashion & Technology Summit in 2017: Trends of Tomorrow. Since June 2017 Luisa Via Roma launched 24 LVR Editions, they release two collaborations per month via only their online store: Sergio Rossi; Dolce & Gabbana; Dilara Findikoglu; Superga;Italia Independent; Angel Chen; Missoni; Marina Hoermanseder; Rene Caovilla; Alberta Ferretti; Lelo; Atlantic Stars; EmanueleFerrariStudio; Qeeboo; Invicta; Marco De Vincenzo; Krizia; Marc Jacques Burton; LVLXIII Jason DeRulo; Dim Mak by Steve Aoki; Alexandre Vauthier; Elie Saab; EA7; Dsquared2.

1) How was the collaboration announced?

LVR Editions are an ongoing series of exclusive collaborations between LuisaViaRoma and international brands and influential industry Figures which aims to promote co-branded limited-edition products and co-branded content, targeting a contemporary audience by offering something exclusive and engaging. From 2010 – 2017, LuisaViaRoma used to do a big party in Florence during Pitti Immagine Uomo named Firenze Forever.

However, from June 2017 we completely changed our strategy to become more international and started doing co-branding collaborations. It's been a year that LVR does co-branding collaborations with different brands, on average LVR does two collaborations per month.

2) What did LuisaViaRoma expect from these monthly collaboration(s)?

Our new concept of doing on average two collaborations per month with international brands helped our brand internationalize at a fast rhythm. We work with international brands and as a result we can plan events in different areas in the world. Our objective is to promote co-branded limited-edition products aimed at an audience that is interested in exclusive, unique, and outstanding products. We do not aim to sell our items at a higher price, which we could due to the items' exclusiveness, but rather to create unique, affordable pieces.

For us, character and individuality are the most important factors that drive trends today. We have understood that success is not derived from being the most famous or most important, but rather from creating and building something that has not been done before. Our mission is to do this when creating a collaboration whilst working with upcoming artists or well-established luxury brands such as Dolce & Gabbana and Alberta Ferreti.

Our monthly collaborations are launched via our website – along with a website launch we engage in events and press events in order to communicate the project with even a wider audience. Our collaborations also have a countdown associated to them. We will for instance start the countdown on a Monday and release the project on a Friday. LuisaViaRoma hopes to make, through collaborations, products that represent a union between two brands.

3) What did this partnership(s) bring to Luisa Via Roma?

Our LVR editions make our brand stand out as we create unexpected emotional collaborations that captivate our consumers. The first co-branded product sold through LVR was with the luxury brand, Sergio Rossi. The product created was a pair of eccentric shoes and it was quickly sold out. Following Sergio Rossi was Dolce & Gabanna. The collection of the LVR & Dolce & Gabbana consisted of four products – trainers, t-shirt, headband, and a wristband. Like the Sergio Rossi collaboration, the Dolce & Gabbana collaboration sold out the same day the products were released.

Our temporary, exclusive partnerships also give our brand an image of luxury and exclusivity. Today, the definition of luxury is evolving – we have understood that luxury today is exclusivity. Owning a piece that is not produced in mass, but rather is limited, has become luxury. In this case, our co-branding is perfect as it meets the exact criteria of today's modern luxury – small production hence limited pieces. For each co-branding collaboration, we produce between 30–100 products only – this is a very limited amount. Hence, owning one of our products provides one with automatic luxury due to our exclusivity.

Our exclusivity makes our co-branded products luxurious and also unique. Our mission is for our co-branded products featured on our e-store to be so unique and creative that the customer has the sensation that he/she is visiting an art exhibition online. As Andrea Panconesi states, "we want the LuisaViaRoma experience to be somewhere between luxury shopping and visiting an art exhibition."

Our partnerships with good causes also help us give back through fashion and better our public image. Partnerships with UNICEF, OXFAM, and Save the Children have all contributed to adding purpose to fashion. In June 2015 our top designers came together to dress an unlikely pop-culture Figure – My Little Pony – for a good cause. LuisaViaRoma put together the impressive line-up as part of an auction for Save the Children' s Nepal earthquake appeal. In April 2015, we also led a campaign against poverty and worldwide injustice. We teamed up with the brand CO Altreforme, a furniture company, and designers such as Manish Arora, Yaz Bukey, corto Moltedo, Fausto Puglisi and KTZ for a collaboration in support of OXFAM Italy. This partnership collection called Altreforme Goes Fashion collection features reimagined versions of the iconic Salvador Chair.

4) What were the fruits of the collaboration and what did it finally bring to LuisaViaRoma?

The way in which we do our collaborations stands out from other collaborations due to our marketing procedure, our fast pace work rhythm, and our communication methods. Our collaborations usually re-emphasize the uniqueness of our brand and our desire to produce never seen material that attracts and captivates large crowds. Due to our work and our resulting co-branded products, our brand is seen as an innovative, international, and successful one.

Communication is a key factor in the success of our co-branding. We communicate via social media platforms such as Instagram posts, specific newsletters for our clients, and we send press releases and communication activities around the launch. Our communication project is also fast pace; we do all the communication activities in one week. Our collaboration functions are up on our online store until all items are sold out.

We also work with a lot of influencers in order to publicize our brand. When we launch products on Wednesdays, we ask influencers to post about our products. We have a close in-house team along with our out of house influencers. Our in-house team consists of stylists, producers, video makers, and photographers.

5) Overall, what were the best parts of the partnership?

LuisaViaRoma invested time (more than a decade) into building an extensive network of digital influencers who have played a fundamental role in connecting with millennials. As a result, LuisaViaRoma is able to keep up with the demands of its audience.

The best parts of our various partnerships through our LVR Editions is the fact that we attract such a wide age group. We manage to have a very mixed audience due to the fact that we have so many different collaborations.

Evidently, the best part of our partnerships are the success rates of them. Our collaborations tend to be sold out very rapidly and hence represent how popular and appreciated our work is.

6) What do you believe were the keys of success of this partnership?

We function at a very high pace and are very effective workers. For instance, we do not plan our collaborations far in advance. We usually plan these activities one or two months in advance. For instance, with our partnership with Dolce & Gabbana, we discussed two weeks before as they have a really quick production and we managed to do it. We are very fast at producing our collaborations since we have a precise format. When we partnered with Superga, our co-branded product was implemented in around three weeks and most of our partnerships are done in around the same time span.

Our fast partnerships are also a contributing factor to the success of our partnerships – as they are temporary short collaborations it is very interactive and attracts consumers. The fact that we do co-branded collaborations and that we have a logo for this project, a bright LVR logo that is placed on all the items makes us stand out. LVR believes that the best co-brandings and collaborations are the ones that are unexpected – something that was never seen before, something that is completely new.

7) What parts of the partnership could have been improved?

For now, we only have an e-store, however, we are thinking of expanding and having an actual store. We are planning at the end of 2018 or the beginning of 2019 to open a new shop in Florence with a specific section for the LVR projects. Our idea is to keep some of the special editions and sell them in our shop.

Image 1.13 *LVR & Italia independent*

Image 1.14 *LVR & Missoni*

Image 1.15 *LVR & Atlantic Stars*

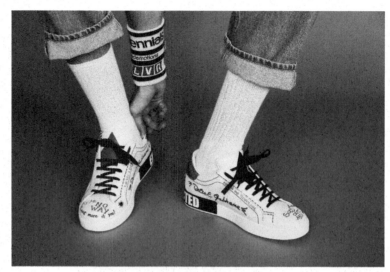

Image 1.16 *LVR & Dolce & Gabbana*

Image 1.17 *LVR & Dolce & Gabbana*

INTERVIEW WITH SÉBASTIEN SERVAIRE

CEO, Founder and Creative Director of the design agency, Servaire & Co.

"Brands should be more daring when doing collaborations"

Keyword: Well balanced

Actors: Servaire & Co.

Servaire & Co. is a global design agency specialized in product, packaging, retail and merchandising design and known for shaking up the rules by creating iconic and smart ideas for brands. Awarded best designer of the year by 2018 Pentawards, the agency won multiple design awards for collaborations with brands such as Veuve Clicquot, diptyque paris, Louis Vuitton, Calvin Klein, Dom Pérignon, Dolce & Gabbana, Hennessy, Lancôme, as well as limited-edition products/collaborations with artists such as Laolu Senbanjo, Jean-Paul Gaultier, Alber Elbaz, Vincent Le Roy, and many others …

1) What is Servaire's role during collaborations?

I like to think of my agency as a facilitator in the design process of collaborations. Many brands do collaborations, but these need to be consistent and meaningful for the brand, and that is where we, as a design agency, play our part. Our goal is to create accessible designed products for the end consumers. When we work with our clients (brands) to co-create together with an artist or personality for a limited-edition product, we put ourselves in the artist's shoes and wear the brand's jacket. The artist needs to feel free to share his/her opinions and artistic inputs more easily. We then orchestrate between us, the artist, and the brand until the final limited-edition design is in line with the brand's vision.

2) How does the creative process of co-brandings and limited editions work on your agency side?

When we design a cobranded product together with the brands and an artist, the brand usually takes care of the artist selection (sometimes we are also consulted throughout this process). Once the artist is picked up, we receive the design brief of our client, and we do a first outline of our creative input, which we send to the brand, who shares it with the artist. Counting the technical studies, the creation, the project updates, it takes up to 18 months to two years when we do such collaborative projects between an artist and a brand.

3) Overall, what are the best parts of collaborations?

Co-branding is fun! The brand can experiment new things, innovate, "tell a story" and by doing so, create a close relationship with its end consumers. When you are two, you're stronger – but both partners have to agree, and understand each other. Another nice part of collaborations is when the brand enables the artist to meet physically with its customers, to experience the brand and sign some of its limited-edition products, or capsule collection. These kinds of events always meet a great success and are well shared on social media too!

4) What are the most difficult parts of collaborations?

A difficult part in a partnership is to go deep enough. In general, I find that brands don't go as far as they should or could go when collaborating with artists. Artists and brands are enthusiastic and want something fun, but at the end it often ends up that we all are too well-behaved and did not dare enough. We did not dare to go further and really innovate for our end consumer, while innovation could generate another layer of appeal to the collaborations than its PR and communication purposes.

5) What do you believe are the keys of success when a brand does collaborations/limited editions?

A brand partnering with a third-party should always think beyond the activation purpose, and the creative outcome of a collaboration. A beautiful limited edition can be achieved without the help of an artist, and at a lower cost! What matters is to make sure that the encounter between the brand and the artist opens new territories for the brand, and also try to take the most out of it: it is not only about a beautiful packaging and a good media plan, it is also about how to generate very strong PR-ability, amplification on a viral communication strategy that will ideally increase the customers involvement and surprise!

REFERENCES

Arnett, D.B., Laverie, D.A. and Wilcox, J.B. (2010). A longitudinal examination of the effects of retailer-manufacturer brand alliances: The role of perceived fit. *Journal of Marketing Management*, 26(1–2), 5–27.

Cegarra, J.J. and Michel, G. (2001). Co-branding: *Clarification du concept. Recherche et Applications en Marketing*, 16(4), 57–69,

Desai, K.K. and Keller, K.L. (2002). The effects of ingredient branding strategies on host brand extendibility. *Journal of Marketing*, 66(1), 73–93.

Erevelles, S., Stevenson, T.H., Srinivasan, S. and Fukawa, N. (2008). An analysis of B2B ingredient co-branding relationships. *Industrial Marketing Management*, 37(8), 940–952.

Hégner, N. and Peixoto, G. (2017). Can brands have superheroes? Master's Thesis, Norwegian School of Economics, Supervisor Preinar Breivik.

Kalafatis, S.P., Ledden, L., Riley, D. and Singh, J. (2016). The added value of brand alliances in higher education. *Journal of Business Research*, 69(8), 3122–3132.

Michel, G. (2017). *Au Coeur de la Marque, les Clés du Management de la Marque*, 3rd edition. Malakoff: Dunod.

Moon, H. and Sprott, D.E. (2016). Ingredient branding for a luxury brand: The role of brand and product fit. *Journal of Business Research*, 69(12), 5768–5774.

Nabec, L., Pras, B. and Laurent, G. (2016). Temporary brand–retailer alliance model: The routes to purchase intentions for selective brands and mass retailers. *Journal of Marketing Management, 32*, 595–627.

Naidoo, V. and Hollebeek, L.D. (2016). Higher education brand alliances: Investigating consumers' dual-degree purchase intentions. *Journal of Business Research, 69*(8), 3113–3121.

CHAPTER 2

Brand collaborations with artists

rands and artists, scandalous wedding or happy marriage? The
association of these two worlds seems unclear. However, in this ever
more "aestheticized" world (Lipovetski, 2013), brands have realized early
on what symbolic benefit they can derive from their relationship with the
art world: it allows them to nurture their desirability and cultivate their
differentiation. For this, they create and maintain relationships with artists
in many ways (artistic foundations, artist residencies, artists' sponsorships).
Collaboration of brands with the arts is not new. Poster artists like Henri
Toulouse-Lautrec (French painter and poster maker) worked in the context
of brand communication. However, the collaboration between brands and
artists has become more diverse: Louis Vuitton & Yayoi Kusama (Japanese
multidisciplinary artist) or Hennessy V.S. Limited Edition by Shepard
Fairey (American street artist). Moreover, brands are collaborating with
artists in order to promote their corporate social responsibility as well
as branding in the company (Antal and Strauß, 2013). Nowadays brands
and artists engage in an act of co-creation giving value to consumers and
enriching the brand identity (Michel and Borraz, 2016). Although the art is
more available, it is still associated with the status of "connoisseurs," with
very expensive prices. In this context, luxury brands are happy to open up
this world to the happy fans willing to buy, for instance, a limited-edition
bag stamped Louis Vuitton & Jeff Koons (American artist) which was
made available for a few thousand dollars before also becoming a piece of
art. In this sense, dealing with art means, for luxury brands, dealing with
something which is positively associated with culture, creativity, tradition,
and rarity (Codignola and Rancati, 2016).

We consider here the collaboration between a brand and an artist when it is based on the artwork of the artist (paint, song, photography, literature, movie, etc.). For instance, if a brand collaborates with Madonna, integrating her musical artistic work, it is considered as a collaboration with an artist but if the collaboration is based only on her image, using only her awareness, it is considered as a collaboration with a celebrity. The brand collaboration with an artist can generate a co-branded product or an experience dedicated to consumers or employees (see Table 2.1).

Table 2.1 Brand collaborations with artists

Kinds of collaboration	Definition	Examples
Co-branded products	Collaboration between a brand and an artist involving a co-definition and a co-naming of a new product	- Uniqlo & Andy Warhol - Louis Vuitton & Jeff Koons - Absolut & Magdiel Lopez - Ipanema & Starck - Kiehl's & Kate Moross
Co-branded event	Collaboration between a brand and an artist involving the creation of a common experience (including events, pop-up stores, etc.)	- Galeries Lafayette & André Saraiva - Bon Marché & Ai Weiwei - Louis XIII & Pharell Williams - Louis XIII & John Malkovish
Brand collaborations dedicated to employees	Collaboration between a brand and an artist involving a specific creation dedicated to employees from the brand's company	- Colas & Lee Bae - Colas & Rafal Olbinski - Bic & Yousef and Elias Anastas, Yann Santerre and Landolf Rhode-Barbarigos

2.1 WHEN BRANDS CREATE PRODUCTS WITH ARTISTS

The collaboration between a brand and an artist allows them to create a new product showing the brand values and the universe of the artist. The champagne brand Dom Pérignon did not hesitate to ask Jeff Koons (American artist) to revisit the bottle of *Balloon Venus*, providing a limited collection. However, the new product with the artistic touch is not enough. Nowadays, collaboration between a brand and an artist needs to highlight the meaning of the artist's work. The Desperados limited bottle of beer illustrates this kind of co-creation. A new label has been revisited each year for almost 20 years by an artist. For the nineteenth collaboration, Desperados beer and Théo Lopez (a French painter) pushed the boundaries of artistic creation. Beyond the label he designed, the artist imagined an experience that allowed people to explore his work through virtual reality. Animations are offered in supermarkets and in a selection of bars with virtual reality headsets that explore the canvas in a three-dimensional space. And this brand-artist collaboration makes sense, thanks to the orchestration of a story told around the roots of Desperados. Again, in the alcohol sector, La Maison Rémy Martin is putting art in the spotlight with a unique collaboration with Matt W. Moore (an American painter). Sharing the values of nature, innovation, and time, the artist transposes the traditional Rémy Martin cognac know-how into a modern setting with its iconic abstract graphics. This performance is remarkable in its innovation and in its uniqueness as an art work in itself.

In the same vein, Rémy Martin collaborated with Vincent Leroy, a renowned French artist, to create limited-edition bottles. The goal was to attract cognac lovers and new targets in search of valorization. Based on the colors of the vine, Vincent Leroy has created an artistic work that has allowed Rémy Martin to offer a unique and inspiring bottle.

Image 2.1 *Rémy Martin & Matt W. Moore*

Image 2.2 *Rémy Martin & Matt W. Moore*

Some brands build their identity around their collaboration with artists. For instance, the Vodka brand Absolut associates its name with modern works of art. Starting with Andy Warhol (an American artist), the bottle Absolut was painted in black by the pop-art artist in 1985 and each year the collection "Absolut Art" integrates a new collaboration. The "Absolut Warhol" ad was significant because it began a relationship between vodka and the arts that continued for decades. More than five hundred artists, including Helmut Newton (a German-Australian photographer), Keith Haring (an American painter), Kenny Scharf (an American painter)

Image 2.3 *Rémy Martin & Vincent Leroy*

and Damian Hirst (a British artist), continue the tradition. If painters, sculptors, stylists, crystal makers, photographers, architects, jewelers, musicians and fashion designers have all creative freedom, they are bound by a golden rule: the bottle remains at the heart of the creation.

In the fashion sector, numerous brands collaborate with artists in designing limited Capsule collections creating uniqueness and exclusivity. Gucci has teamed up with the young Spanish artist Ignasi Monreal to create a limited-edition line-up of nine T-shirts and sweatshirts. Only 200 T-shirts

Image 2.4 *Absolut & Trockel*

bearing the artist's illustrations will be produced, and each illustration will be printed on 100 sweatshirts. All will have a unique number, like a limited edition in the art world. Adding a special touch is the packaging, which will feature the artist's work. This collaboration was orchestrated by the #GucciHallucination campaign.

The most recognizable brand collaboration between a brand and an artist, in the fashion sector, is the one of Louis Vuitton and Jeff Koons (an American artist). Louis Vuitton has a longstanding collaborative history with iconic artists such as Stephen Sprouse (an American artist) who designed the graffiti bags. Its latest collaboration with Jeff Koons presents paintings that are reproductions of works by the greats (Da Vinci, Van Gogh, Titian, Fragonard, and Rubens) transposed onto Louis Vuitton's most well-known bags: the Speedy, the Neverfull, and the Keepall. This collaboration is outstanding because, through the range of handbags, rucksacks, and other expensive accessories, Koons is turning great art back into popular culture. For the artist it's an important platform for communication – they can put their work in the street! For Jeff Koons, this is part of his mission statement as an artist: he wants to eradicate the elitism of the art world. On the other hand, the brand Louis Vuitton is enriching the Louis Vuitton brand identity as an avant-garde spirit. In the end, consumers are being introduced to great art and, partly to encourage this, Vuitton and Mr. Koons have added a subnarrative to the project that spins it as an effort to address the falling profile of classical art. Inside each bag, for example, lies a little description of the artist, like a hidden history lesson for the Twitter generation. The art paintings are all in the public domain – hence these collaborations have the support of the museums looking to reviving a classic art. This collaboration is positive for the three stakeholders; however, it got a bad buzz in the social media. The consumers did not appreciate the bag design showing Old Master paintings and thought they were untasteful. Louis Vuitton believed its collaboration imposed its unique style and Jeff Koons affirmed "I think these bags are art works."

The collab was not recieved well. what are the reasons behind it?

Image 2.5 *LV & Jeff Koons & Van Gogh*

Image 2.6 *LV & Jeff Koons & Monet*

Image 2.7 *LV & Jeff Koons & Fragonard*

In order to prove their values, the famous Brazilian brand Ipanema teamed up with the artist designer Philippe Starck for a collaboration named "listening to the Earth." The shoes from the capsule collection "Ipanema with Starck" have two advantages: they are modern and environment friendly. Thirty per cent of the components are produced with recyclable materials and the shoes are 100% recyclable.

In the food and alcohol markets, numerous brands work with artists creating limited collections. Each year Evian introduces a new limited edition collector series of bottles with artists such as Japanese fashion designer Issey Miyake, who drew a flower inspired by his innovative pleated clothes. This kind of limited collection stimulates the rejuvenation of the brand and attracts consumers looking for pleasure in their daily purchases.

Image 2.8 *LV & Jeff Koons & Vinci*

CONSUMER TESTIMONY

Frédéric, 50-years-old, single, sales director, French, SMEG (Italian domestic appliance brand) & Dolce & Gabbana (interviewed in December 2018)

I live in a cosy and warm flat in Paris. It's quite big, especially for the capital city. I have several rooms and a big kitchen. I wanted to have a decoration that was in line with my taste of course, but also something sophisticated with furniture that could create admiration. I have got my Starck chairs in the living room and an ancient Chinese jar in the bedroom. I have got some paintings on the walls and modern, industrial-like lights. When it came to the kitchen, I was disappointed by the possibilities. I wanted at least one thing that could pop out when entering the room. When I found out that SMEG did a collection of a few fridges with Dolce & Gabbana, it seemed to me that it was the perfect addition to my home. I saw them at first in a shop in London. I looked carefully, trying to understand the depicted scenes and to differentiate each one of them. As every fridge displayed was unique, it was hard to decide. The artistic pattern and the very sophisticated, yet warm and understandable aspect of the fridge helped me make my decision. I really don't regret it. Of course, it was very expensive but it sure makes a difference! My other designer furniture is totally left behind when compared to this piece. I was happy to buy a SMEG product as it's a brand I trust, and even more satisfied to get an artistic turn on such a usually sad product.

2.2 WHEN BRANDS OFFER EXPERIENCES WITH ARTISTS

When brands collaborate with artists it is not only to launch a new product but it can also to create an experience in a commercial space or to create an event for a specific occasion.

1) CO-BRANDED EVENTS IN STORES

Art has been present in different brands' stores for several decades now. For 15 years, since 2001, the department store Galeries Lafayette, founded in 1893, has devoted part of its first floor to exhibitions of contemporary art. These exhibitions are conceptually demanding, but they remain accessible to all, both experts and neophytes. Half of the visitors come only for the exhibitions. These partnerships between department stores and artists increase the attractiveness and the number of visits of consumers. Moreover, Galeries Lafayette's support for a younger generation of artists gives it an influential role in the world of art that adds a creative touch to its fashion image (for example, the French street artists André, and Jean-Paul Goude). For their part, the artists benefit from high visibility in a place of high footfall which allows them to reach a public different from that of the museums.

Culture and shopping match well. Moreover, one of Galerie Lafayette's competitors, the department store Printemps, transformed spaces into an art gallery to highlight fashion, art and design creations. Thus, Le Printemps in the Louvre gallery exhibited XXL works by five international artists: Gilles Cenazandotti (a French sculptor), Kordian Lewandowski (a Polish sculptor), Matt Maitland (a British visual artist), Wang Qiang (a Chinese artist), and Gao Yu (a Chinese painter), who gave the handbag a pop vision. By exhibiting canvases or photos, contemporary art invites itself into department stores. The art works are not for sale but customers can admire them while shopping. The clientele, curious and interested, who do not dare to cross the door of museums, appreciates it a lot. At Le Bon Marché, another competitor, a contemporary art acquisition fund was created in 1990 and since then the collection continues to grow. No less than 80 art works are on display, such as Leandro Erlich's (an Argentinian artist). Shopping and museum merge into one. All these examples are summed up in the words of pop art hero Andy Warhol who said, in 1975, "all museums will become department stores and all department stores will become museums."

Retailers are increasingly entering into brand alliances with artists, but the conditions under which such alliances are most effective are not clear. A recent survey shows both the positive and the negative effects of these collaborations (Kim et al., 2018b). It demonstrates that the retailer's brand personality is expanded when the artist has a personality moderately consistent with the retailer's brand, while it is diluted when the visual artist has a personality strongly inconsistent with the identity of the retailer. These findings suggest visual artists are an untapped source of value that retailers can exploit to create differentiated brand personalities as a way to gain greater market appeal.

Also, in the context of store atmospherics, incorporating artistic elements into a store constitutes an innovative way for retailers to differentiate their shopping experience (Vukadin, Lemoine, and Badot, 2016). They can

Image 2.9 *le bon marché & Erlich*

maximize hedonic gratification for store visitors, while adding symbolic
value to the commercial offering. Incorporating artistic elements is also a
magical way to conceal the store's transactional purpose. Indeed, through
this association with the art world, the store is viewed as less mercantile.
However, be carefull there is a risk that consumers will view the store as a
"museum" and visit without purchasing.

2) CO-BRANDED EVENTS FOR SPECIFIC OCCASIONS

Beyond the commercial space, brands collaborate with artists to offer a unique experience for their clients. For the eighty-fifth anniversary, the iconic brand Zippo asked the artist Ben Eine (a British street artist) to create the world's largest street art work. The realization of the work took more than 500 hours, with six artists and 30 volunteers. More than 2,850 litres of recycled paint were used. The collaboration between Zippo and the artist makes sense, as the work inspired the launch of a limited-edition lighter. For 85 years the brand has put forward unparalleled artistic talent on their lighters. This partnership with Ben Eine highlights the diversity of the Zippo range of lighters and enriches the symbolic universe of an iconic brand. In another context, on the occasion of the launch of the new design of its range of shopping bags, the French retailer Edouard Leclerc collaborated with the artist JonOne, an American painter and graphic designer, to illustrate six different bags. Within this collaboration, Edouard Leclerc purchased the exclusive rights to five works of art, which are reproduced on the distributor's bags for the benefit of the Abbé-Pierre Foundation (an NGO defending the poorest in our society). This example shows how the partnership between brands and artists can bring sense to the brand and seduce consumers, mixing art and the support of good causes.

In another vein, the spirit brand, Louis XIII, has created two artistic works to highlight the 100 years of their cognac production process. The cognac brand, Louis XIII, has collaborated with actor John Malkovich and director Robert Rodriguez to create a film that will only be seen in a century – a century refers to the time it took four generations of Cellar Masters to develop Louis XIII Cognac. The movie "You Will Never See" will be released in November 18, 2115. In order to ensure that the "100 Years" remains intact until its official release, the film will be placed in a strongbox made in partnership with Fichet-Bauche (a French brand of safes). The custom safe is made of armoured glass and equipped with a timer displaying the time and date and counting down the next 100 years. Again to highlight the time needed to produce the cognac, Louis XIII has just collaborated with Pharrell Williams (an American singer) to create a song entitled "100 Years: The Song We'll Only Hear if We Care." An original musical work composed by the artist, it will only be possible to listen it in 2117. As both concerned about the environment, Louis XIII joined Pharrell Williams in the idea of raising awareness about global warming. "100 Years: The Song We'll Only Hear If We Care" was unveiled at a private event in Shanghai, where only 100 VIP guests could listen to the song without being able to record it. The disc has now been placed in a safe in the House of Louis XIII and can only be listened to if the trunk has not been immersed in water due through climate change. This kind of collaboration expresses its brand values and creates a buzz around the Louis XIII brand as a symbol of innovation and creativity.

In terms of image, the collaboration of the brands with the contemporary art scene makes it possible to show that one understands one's time, because it speaks about creativity, innovation, impertinence, and disruption. It was totally within the spirit of Le Louvre museum when they accepted a collaboration with Beyoncé (an American R&B singer) and Jay-Z (American hip hop singer). The singers shoot a video, for their song APES T, from their album "Everything is Love," in the museum of Le Louvre. The clip lets us see several major paintings from the permanent collection – The Mona Lisa of Vinci, The Marriage of Cana of Veronese, The Rite of Napoleon by Jacques-Louis David – and works less known to the general public – The Officer of Chasseurs on horseback of Géricault, the statue of Hermès attaching his sandal, the Portrait of a black woman of Marie-Guillemine Benoist. Beyond the video, the museum offers a list of the 17 works used as references in their clip. For the museum, the operation is already a success. A month after its release, the video has been seen by more than 80 million people and the brand Le Louvre has earned a "cooler" image. This partnership has made sense for the brand Le Louvre who exploited this visibility to stimulate visits from younger people who feel removed from classical art. Finally, the video of Beyoncé and Jay-Z at Le Louvre addresses the challenge faced by the great museums – the need to gain exposure and to get people to talk about it.

These examples show that when seeking to attract a new target segment, brands can ally with artists who convey a personality that matches that of the new target segment (d'Astou et al., 2007; Kim et al., 2018a).

2.3 WHEN BRANDS AND ARTISTS COLLABORATE TO TARGET EMPLOYEES

Just as brands create value for customers, they also create value for employees – the brand is a social object giving sense to employees. Specifically, the brand creates a triad of qualities – signification, direction, and sensation – for employees. A corporate brand or a commercial brand gives meaning to work through significations expressed in the form of a common good, professional pride, and job security. It contributes to brand identity through constructed social utility and congruence of values with the long-term point of view. Lastly, it provides sensations through emotional attachment and the feeling of pride due to the outside image projected (Berger-Remy and Michel, 2015). To increase the value created by the brand, it is important to encourage employees to become close to the brand, even those not naturally in contact with the brand in their profession.

The company can, for example, bring in works of art related to the company's businesses into the workplace, which improves employees' everyday lives by providing them with meaning. For instance, the international brand Bic, well-known for its pens, lighters, and razors, shows the works from artists using Bic pens or other products from the company in the corridors of the company. The Bic collaboration with architects/engineers (Yousef and Elias Anastas, Yann Santerre) and a research laboratory (Landolf Rhode-Barbarigos in the university of Miami) can also bring pride to employees when they see the unique artist work designed and realized with 12,843 Bic pens and exhibited in the main hall of the Saint Lazard train station in Paris. Also, the leader of construction, Colas Foundation supports many artists around the world with an original approach. Every year, a selection committee selects about 15 professional painters of different nationalities. The laureates must then make a canvas inspired by the theme of the road. For the Colas group, this collaboration with artists, such as Lee Bae (a South Korean artist) or Rafal Olbinski (a Polish painter), is an integral part of internal communication. It strengthens the cohesion, identity, and pride of belonging to the company. The art works of the Foundation travel – they are displayed in offices, public spaces, and reception areas at headquarters and subsidiaries, in France and abroad. Their variety is representative of the cultural and social diversity of the company and gives meaning to the mission of the company and the jobs of employees. As explained by the management of the company, "Every collaborator must find himself/herself in the works that are made."

These employer brand-artist partnerships are part of a social responsibility approach. It is useful to specifically embody the brand values in works of art to give meaning to employees, going beyond the halo effects of advertisements designed for the general public. Art is a lever of performance in terms of human resources. These artist-brand collaborations show that the company is able to grow its employees outside the usual realms of work by bringing them creativity and meaning within their work (Antal, Debucquet and Frémeaux, 2018).

TRANSCEND POTENTIAL MISCONCEPTIONS

- It is not necessary to choose an artist who shares the brand's values – rather choose an artist who creates more than a new packaging, choose an artist who goes beyond the product and the brand values to create new ideas.
- A brand collaboration allows the brand to experiment with new things in a way it could not do alone. The artist brings a space of creativity. When a brand takes the risk of challenging its register of values, it provides inspiration and lives longer.
- The events during which the artist creates or dedicates a limited quantity of works are important because, beyond the art work, the artist creates a meaningful experience.
- Brand-artist collaborations do not only create value for consumers, they also enable employees to embody the brand values and to be committed to the vision of the company.

LOUIS XIII
Rémy Martin
COGNAC GRANDE CHAMPAGNE

INTERVIEW WITH LUDOVIC DU PLESSIS
Global Executive Director of Louis XIII Cognac

"When celebrities talk about your product naturally"

Keywords: organic endorsement, think a century ahead

Actors: Louis XIII, John Malkovich, Pharrell Williams

Louis XIII is a cognac, produced by Rémy Martin, a company headquartered in Cognac.

Think a century ahead. Each decanter of Louis XIII is the life achievement of generations of cellar masters. Since its origins in 1874, each generation of cellar master selects from our cellars the oldest and most precious eaux-de-vie for Louis XIII. Today, Cellar Master Baptiste Loiseau is setting aside our finest eaux-de-vie as a legacy to his successors for the coming century. Louis XIII is an exquisite blend of up to 1,200 eaux-de-vie sourced 100% from Grande Champagne, the first cru of the Cognac region. The legendary decanters have been made from fine crystal for generations, mouth-blown by some of the most skilled master craftsmen. Louis XIII features exceptional aromas evoking myrrh, honey, dried roses, plum, honeysuckle, cigar box, leather, figs, and passion fruit.

John Malkovich is a 64-year-old, renowned American actor, director and producer who has appeared in over 70 films. He was spotted by Spielberg who gave him the main role in his movie "Empire of the Sun." He is known as one of the most brilliant actors of his generation.

Pharrell Williams is a 45-year-old American singer and record producer. Williams has earned ten Grammy Awards. He was nominated twice for an Academy Award and nominated in 2014 for Best Original Song with his successful single "Happy" which has over a billion views on YouTube.

1) How did Louis XIII decide to announce the collaborations?

For both collaborations we invited our VIP guests to high-end previews! In 2015, Louis XIII partnered with renowned actor and creative visionary John Malkovich to create "100 Years: The Movie You Will Never See," a thought-provoking artistic work that explores the relationship of past, present, and future. For the preview of John Malkovich's movie, we invited our privileged guests to Los Angeles where we showed the trailer of Malkovich's movie, only the trailer. After that, the only copy of the movie was put in a safe that we closed in front of the guests for the next 100 years. When we closed the door, it started a timer, a countdown integrated to the safe. In 100 years, the 13 November 2115, it will open automatically. There is no code, no key to open the safe, only the time will open it. Every guest was given an invitation for his descendants to attend the movie projection in 2115. The movie is conceived as a short film, depicting a number of possible futures depending on the actions of mankind on our planet earth. Our guests were invited to use the hashtag #notcomingsoon.

In 2017, Louis XIII announced "100 Years" a new song by Pharrell Williams to be released in 2117, only #ifwecare. Pharrell's exclusive track has been recorded onto a record made of clay from the chalky soil of Cognac and stored in the cellars of Louis XIII in a state-of-the-art safe specially designed by Fichet-Bauche that is destroyed when submerged in water. If sea levels continue to rise at such an alarming rate due to climate change, scientists project that in 100 years a significant portion of the world's land might be underwater. The only way to guarantee this original piece of music will be heard again in 2117, one century from now, is if we address the tragic consequences of global warming – if we do not change our way of living, future generations will never be able to hear this song. "100 Years" by Pharrell Williams will be out in 2117, but only #Ifwecare."100 Years" was premiered during a private listening party in Shanghai, where

Pharrell presented the song, one time only. The one hundred lucky guests in attendance have not been allowed to record the once-in-a-lifetime experience, so the song remains a secret for the next century. Louis XIII and Pharrell aim to inspire these guests to take action and motivate others to get involved in the international effort to curb global warming. This project is an exciting creative exploration of the way our actions today shape the world of tomorrow. Nature and time are at the heart of what we do – each decanter of Louis XIII represents the life achievement of generations of Cellar Masters, so Louis XIII must always think a century ahead. If the environment is unstable, even the greatest cellar masters would not be able to compose the exceptional blend that is Louis XIII.The 100 VIPs were each given a silver ticket to pass on to their future generations to come listen to the single in a hundred years' time, in 2117.

2) What were Louis XIII's expectations for the partnerships?

These two collaborations were a tribute to the long-standing relationship of Louis XIII with time. Our aim was to enhance people's understanding of the time-bounded experience they have by drinking Louis XIII. We want them to understand what time means. The VIP guest we invited for both our preview events in Los Angeles and Shanghai were "our friends," and they became "ambassadors" of our artistic projects by posting their pictures and comments on our exceptional, once in a lifetime event! We invited the most famous actors, singers, personalities worldwide. All were truly excited to be part of such an original event with repercussions in 100 years for their own descendants!

Our first collaboration was with cinema as everyone loves cinema … and so music is introducing our second partnership. The collaboration with Pharrell went even further, as we promoted next to time an issue dear to our hearts, global warming. "100 years, the song we'll only hear if we care," is the creative expression of the delicate relationship between nature and time, and the effect humans have on their environment. The single will never be released, and it will decompose underwater if we don't change our habits. Hence, we launched the hashtag #ifwecare, expecting people to start caring if they want to hear the song. We challenge the world to stop global warming! We are organizing events in big cities throughout the globe where the safe is travelling to, to collect money for environmental charities. It also helps to make people aware that our cognac is made in vineyards that are very sensitive to weather conditions and the soil.

3) What did this partnership bring to both personalities?

Pharrell and John were both really intrigued and loved the concept of a 100 years' wait.These collaborations also mean they will be reminded and talked about in 100 years when the project finally comes out. Delayed gratification in a way!

We decided to partner with John Malkovich because he is the best in his generation, he is a Louis XIII lover, and he speaks better French than me! Pharrell is a great musician, he understood directly Louis XIII message. Also, we have a common interest in preserving nature for the future, as he is a huge defender of climate change. Hence, creating a song to defend the environment means a lot to Pharrell.

4) What were the fruits of both collaborations?

We had more than a reach of 700 million and more than 70 million engagements of people who liked, commented or shared on the project. In general, our message about the value of time had a really good response. Time is luxury! And that everybody seems to agree upon! When you drink Louis XIII, you drink time.

5) Who worked on both collaborations?

For the movie, John Malkovich wrote the script himself from A to Z. And the movie was realized by Robert Rodriguez with a casting of only four actors, including John himself as the main character. As for the collaboration with Pharrell Williams, he also composed the song entirely himself. And, of course, the Louis XIII team based in Paris, including myself, worked on both concepts and roll out of both collaborations together with our advertising agency FF.

One important thing is the fact that I said to both John and Pharrell that I will not change a word, a comma of what they create. It is his movie, it is his song. I changed nothing. It is their pure creation. It is not a movie or a song about Louis XIII.

6) Overall, what were the best parts of the creative campaign?

For both campaigns, we worked with people that were truly invested in the project and completely understood what the Louis XIII house was trying to do. The best part is that these collaborations are particularly meaningful for the brand and the celebrities. The best is yet to come as the partnerships are far from being done as it's all about delayed gratification! And we hope to continue doing more collaborations under the same concept!

7) And the more difficult parts of the collaboration?

I believe the most difficult part is to wait.

8) What do you believe where the keys of the success of these two partnerships?

In general, each partnership project needs to be very meaningful. The project won't necessarily succeed if you take a celebrity without a true meaning behind the collaboration.

Louis XIII does not have a huge communication budget so we have to be creative and come up with meaningful ideas.

I think that before starting any partnership, you need to have a stable brand and a strong territory. By this, I mean you must focus on your product first and make sure it's the best in its category, in our case, cognac. Only after, as a second step, you can look at different marketing strategies including collaborations. Hence, I believe that a key of success for us was the stability of the Louis XIII house.

I strongly believe organic endorsement is very efficient. Organic endorsement is having celebrities who will endorse your product naturally. Today, a lot of brands invest in celebrities to talk about their product and, trust me, people realize when money is involved. Hence, if you create a strong network and propose quality products, celebrities will talk about it naturally and that's when people truly get interested and a great success for your brand is assured.

Image 2.10 *Bottle of Louis XIII*

INTERVIEW WITH KENZO TAKADA
Artist and designer

"The most successful collaborations are when a brand gives me Carte Blanche, and trusts my creativity!"

Keyword: the artist knows best

Actors: Kenzo Takada, past 20 years of collaborations

Kenzo Takada is a Japanese fashion designer, born in 1939. He established his fashion house in Paris in the early 70s. He is part of the same generation and as popular as the fashion greats who contributed to the early stages of ready-to-wear such as Karl Lagerfeld, Sonia Rykiel, and Christian Lacroix. He sold his fashion label in 1993 to LVMH and left his artistic direction role in 1999. Recent collaborations include Avon perfume, Roche Bobois, Mandarin Oriental, Baccarat, Coca-Cola, Lipton tea, and many others

1) How did you, Kenzo Takada start to work on collaborations and why?

After retiring from my fashion house in 1999, I quickly realized that I wanted to stay active – but at the same time, I wanted to take a step back from the busy world of fashion, after working non-stop for 30 years. Soon after leaving, I started to receive many collaboration opportunities for various collections from lifestyle brands, to decoration and furniture brands, hotels, to cosmetic, including mass market brands such as Coke or Lipton. All the brands who approached me were looking for a style that I worked with for so many years, bringing joy with a touch of florals and colors. I was probably recognized by most around the world for that!

2) What advice would you as an artist give to another artist, before going into the adventure of doing a collaboration with a brand?

From my perspective, working on collaborations is a great adventure! It's wonderful to meet new people, a new brand with know-how from different fields of expertise. You always learn new things, and it is a new challenge for every new partnership! For instance, with the Avon perfume collaboration (2016) it was fascinating to be involved together with my team, building and making a scent, a bottle, a packaging based on a concept and an idea you would like to push forward. The team of perfumers at Firmenich were translating parts of my personal history and cultural background into a perfume. We were working together bringing various knowledge to make one final product. It's important for me to feel good with the people you're going to work with. If not, it can jeopardize your creativity!

Last, always make sure you approve all designs, all communications, press releases; really anything on which you put your name on or designs should be approved by you before going forward. Its important so you'll have an overall view and make sure all elements tell the same story, making it all coherent. The products you are working on and produce affect the way people see you and your identity.

3) What advice would you give to a brand, when collaborating with a renowned artist like you?

To give the artist carte blanche! The brand may give some indications/ parameters, but shouldn't do the work without the person it is collaborating with. The artist always knows better what works best for the brand in my belief. It is important to listen and learn what the firm is looking for, and if you can bring that to them. Sometimes brands have too specific demands, and the artist loses all his creativity, and does this only to please the commercial/business aspects. I believe the commercial side should be there only to serve creativity and not the contrary. Otherwise, there is no real improvement to the products, and risks are minimized.

Sometimes creating takes time. It happens that very simple things, such as creating a flower for a next advertising campaign, takes me several weeks, because I want it to be perfect. And I need days to restart and restart until I am pleased with the result. Brands often don't understand the creative timings an artist needs to go through … . And they rush into the process with little time to process, making it challenging to come out with the expected result.

Sometimes, I feel that brands often forget that I'm an artist, a designer, and not a public personality, an actor. Brands happen to confuse these two totally different roles and should know who they are looking for, if only looking to endorse a company, but I prefer to design and not speak publicly, for which actors, celebrities excel much better than me. Let's put it this way, I am a terrible marketing tool but a very sensible artist.

4) How do you select the brands/companies you work with and what are your objectives behind these collaborations?

My team receives between two and three requests per month. Sometimes the collaboration demands come from small brands who wish to increase their visibility, others, for instance, Avon, are very big and long-lasting partnerships. We created a perfume together which has been on sale globally since 2016, but we started the project in 2014.

I like to collaborate with mass-market brands but also for more exclusive services and products. Once I understand the added value I can bring, and if the project amuses me, involving to work on design, graphics, colors, florals, and fabrics, I feel most at ease.

Our selection criteria are by order of importance: the quality of the project and its product. If it is in line with my creativity, if it amuses me, if the people we will work with are getting along with my team and trustworthy, then we tend to move forward based on our capacity to respond to the project.

Sometimes we do accept projects when it's for a good cause – like supporting awareness on the Fukushima event or partnering with a brand to help children in Cambodia getting into schools. All in all, since I sold my fashion house, all the many collaborations I have done give me a certain purpose and allow me to work with my team.

5) How do you explain the success of a collaboration?

Some collaborations are only for a very short period – one capsule collection for instance with Lenotre, or Carrefour's textile brand TEX – and others are there for several years. With the furniture brand Roche Bobois our collaboration was such a success that we continued for several years. Most, if not all, of our collaborations have been great successes and some way above expectations. It mainly relies on good teamwork between my team and the partner, working together.

In general, collaborations are great ways for companies to become more creative, and bring exciting new products to the market. It helps them to expand beyond their perceived identity. I love bringing diverse cultures and other influences into my work – this is what the customer perceives and why the product sells well!

6) How do you foresee the future of collaborations?

It is true that for at least ten years we have seen a great increase in brand collaborations. It is a perfect way for brands to tell a new story, a story that can sometimes last for several years. A brand can shape its own identity in different ways, thanks to collaboration; it can surf on the visibility and creativity of the artist it collaborates with. It's a much stronger and relevant tool than just plain advertising! Collaborations are great happenings! In that sense it's an artwork and it speaks for itself!

Image 2.11 *Kenzo Takada*

LABORATOIRE
ARTISTIQUE
DU GROUPE BEL

INTERVIEW WITH LAURENT FIÉVET

Director of Lab'Bel

"Unexpected collaboration between art and cheese, resulting in a contemporary piece of art"

Keyword: collectables

Actors: Lab'Bel, The Laughing Cow®, Wim Delvoye

The Laughing Cow® is the first processed cheese available in individual wedges that could be preserved and easily carried thanks to its unique aluminium wrapped packaging. It is owned by Group Bel and created by Léon Bel in 1921. In 1924, Léon Bel changed the logo to a hilarious red cow with earrings designed by illustrator Benjamin Rabier.

Some figures:

- For generations, The Laughing Cow® has been the number one children's cheese
- Ten million portions sold each day
- Available in 136 countries on five continents
- In France, 97% of children between the ages of seven and 12 and 98% of mothers know the brand
- 1,050,000 Facebook fans

Lab'Bel is the artistic laboratory of the Bel Group, created in 2010 and based on a firm desire on behalf of the industrial group Bel to develop a policy committed to the support and promotion of contemporary art, open and accessible to the general public. It is a laboratory of ideas and innovation that aims to support and contribute to the development of contemporary artistic creation.

Lab'Bel structures its identity around three thematic areas: humour, eclecticism, and impertinence. It has a collection of contemporary art where new acquisitions are added annually and it is currently at the Musée des Beaux-Arts de Dole in the Jura, France.

Wim Delvoye is an internationally renowned artist, born in Wervik, Belgium in 1965. He lives and works in Brighton and is represented by the Galerie Perrotin (Paris, New York, Hong Kong, Seoul, Tokyo). Delvoye's work combines history and art, Flemish tradition and industry in a fashion that is both unsettling and alluring in its inventive richness and indifference to cultural norms. In his juggling of science and popular culture, Wim Delvoye mixes impertinence with formal research through artistic creations that parody both artisanal savoir-faire and scientific research.

1) How was the collaboration announced?

In preparation for the celebration of its100th anniversary in 2021, The Laughing Cow® in 2014 launched a remarkable series of collaborations with renowned contemporary artists for the creation of its exceptional cheese Collector's Edition Box series. Produced annually, four different collector boxes with the Laughing Cow® have been developed with different artists:

- The first one, in 2014, with Hans-Peter Feldmann
- In 2015, the second artist was Thomas Bayrle
- In 2016, then Jonathan Monk
- In 2017, Wim Delvoye and
- In 2018, Karin Sander.

These original projects both fulfil and continue the long-standing relationship between artists and The Laughing Cow®, a modern icon which has served for more than a century as a source of creative and artistic inspiration.

The Collector's Edition boxes are considered by their creators/artists to be original works of art, available to the public for the very affordable price of just €5.

The boxes are limited editions. The one in 2017 launched with just 5,000 copies and was only distributed at the FIAC (International Art Fair) and online. By the way, we were among the biggest art seller at the FIAC with 3,500 Collector's Edition Boxes sold!

2) What were Lab'Bel's expectations for these collaborations?

The main objective for Lab'Bel is to support the contemporary artistic creation through the constitution of a collection and exhibitions. We wanted the collector box of The Laughing Cow® to be reasonably priced. Today, the collector box is €5 which is very affordable knowing how much we put into it. But, overall, all the production costs of the collector box end up being more expensive than the profits we make. It was never our idea to make profit out of our projects. We see it as an investment for the brand as it nourishes its history.

3) What did this partnership bring to the artists you collaborated with?

This collaboration is not very appealing financially wise for the artist as he is not paid much. I guess the artists are sensitive to the goals of the project and its values. The Collector's Edition Boxes project was born out of the desire to shake up ways of looking at contemporary art, its modes of distribution, and the art market through the edition of a very affordable artwork; these principles are really appealing and challenging for the artists. For Wim Delvoye, the collaboration was evident as he is the biggest collector of The Laughing Cow® Labels, of which he has assembled nearly 6,000 pieces. He has a strong link with the brand. The idea is to find a good compromise between a product with a strong identity and the work of the artist, which must be altogether consistent.

4) What were the fruits of the collaboration and what did it finally bring to Lab'Bel?

The collaborations are overall a success. As of today, we have done six different collaborations between artists and The Laughing Cow®.

Since 2014, six artists have successfully participated in the exercise of confronting and integrating the brand and its codes, and all that it has managed to build over time with their own particular practice, and in so doing, shifting its perception. They skilfully responded to the commission from the Group Bel and its Artistic Laboratory by questioning its status and the iconic character of its laughing effigy.

We know that this project will forever stay in the history of the brand. I can say with some degree of confidence that the Group Bel, its employees and directors, but also the family that has been at its head for five generations, are extremely grateful to these artists. Furthermore, we take great pride in these successive collaborations. I allow myself, on their behalf, to extend our warmest thanks.

As for the customer's response, most of the time people take it well and sometimes people will question it. Even if some of them can be critical, we are aware of the value of what we offer to them.

5) Who worked on these collaborations?

Lab'Bel along with The Laughing Cow® corporate teams have worked on the collaborations with the artists. The Laughing Cow® corporate team makes sure the necessary information is on the box – such as nutrients, check if the values and the spirit of the brand are respected and is implied in the choice of the artists at an early stage.

And we, Lab'Bel, the commissioner, are in charge of the whole process from finding the perfect artist that will fit this demand to the launch of the collector box. The commissioner knows exactly the scope of this project – its constraints and the possibilities. We have to find the right balance between the brand's expectations and the artist's work.

6) Overall, what were the best parts of the partnership?

Overall the collector box idea is amazing! Having six different artists who, through art, play with the image of the brand and end up with completely different designs and conceptual approaches is super interesting.

Being part of the FIAC, a manifestation of contemporary art in Paris that takes place once a year, is clearly a highlight and a form of recognition of the quality of our works from the art world. At the FIAC, we share our project, sell the boxes, meet new artists and our collectors.

7) And the more difficult parts of the partnership?

Finding the right balance between Lab'Bel objectives, the Laughing Cow® and Bel Group teams' expectations and the artist's creativity. We need to educate the Laughing Cow® teams – which change regularly – and persuade and convince them with the best arguments.

We can't let the corporate teams interfere in the work of the artists as we can't tell the artist what he must or must not do on the box.

We always make sure to be careful while still taking risks – we have collaborated with some artists who are perceived by some people noxious, like Wim Delvoye, for example.

A difficult part is also the distribution of the box, which I would like to have in supermarkets as well. The first collector box was distributed in supermarkets but after that none. As it is very expensive and complicated to put a new product in supermarkets and causes of a lot of risk financially, we had to stop it. Hence, today, the collector box is only available online and at the FIAC each year. However, we truly hope that the collector box will be distributed again in supermarkets. Our main objective is to give access and offer contemporary art to the public, hence reach a larger audience.

8) What do you believe were the keys of success of these partnerships?

The main key to have a successful partnership it to choose the right artists. For us, the point of this project is not to partner with any well-known artist. We want to find the right artist who will find the right balance between his work and what The Laughing Cow©'s for almost a century. It has to fit.

The relationship between Wim Delvoye and The Laughing Cow® is a rich one which reaches far beyond 2017's artistic partnership. Delvoye is one of the world's foremost collectors of The Laughing Cow® labels, dating from the beginning of the brand in the 1920s and continuing through the present day. He used them in an important piece of art called "After Darwin, on the origin of species," which became quite emblematic in his production.

Image 2.12 *Bel & Wim Delvoye*

REFERENCES

Antal, A.B. and Strauß, A. (2013). Artistic interventions in organisations: Finding evidence of values-added. *Creative Clash Report, WZB.*

Antal, A.B., Debucquet, G. and Frémeaux, S. (2018). Meaningful work and artistic interventions in organizations: Conceptual development and empirical exploration. *Journal of Business Research, 85,* 375–385.

d'Astous, A., Colbert, F. and Fournier, M. (2007). An experimental investigation of the use of brand extension and co-branding strategies, in the arts. *Journal of Services Marketing, 21*(4), 231–240.

Berger-Remy, F. and Michel, G. (2015). How brand gives employees meaning: Towards an extended view of brand equity. *Recherche et Applications en Marketing*, *30*(2), 30–54.

Codignola, F. and Rancati, E. (2016). The blending of luxury fashion brands and contemporary art: A global strategy for value creation. In *Handbook of Research on Global Fashion Management and Merchandising* (pp. 50–76). IGI Global.

Kim, P., Vaidyanathan, R., Chang, H. and Stoel, L. (2018a). Using brand alliances with artists to expand retail brand personality. *Journal of Business Research*, *85*, 424–433.

Kim, P., Chang, H., Vaidyanathan, R. and Stoel, L. (2018b). Artist-Brand alliances to target new consumers: can visual artists recruit new consumers to a brand? *Journal of Product & Brand Management*, *27*(3), 308–319.

Lipovetsky G. (2013). *L'esthétisation du monde. Vivre à l'âge du capitalisme artiste*. Gallimard.

Michel, G. and Borraz S. (2015). *Quand les artistes s'emparent des marques*. Dunod.

Schroeder, J.E. (2005). The artist and the brand. *European Journal of Marketing*, *39*(11/12), 1291–1305.

Vukadin, A., Lemoine, J.F. and Badot, O. (2016). Opportunities and risks of combining shopping experience and artistic elements in the same store: a contribution to the magical functions of the point of sale. *Journal of Marketing Management*, *32*(9–10), 944–964.

CHAPTER 3

Brand collaborations with celebrities

B rands offer speaking time to people who have strong recognition in the public world. Collaborations with celebrities allow brands to convey their values with conviction. Celebrities bring content, they tell the story in a different tone than the brand alone (story-telling). Indeed, celebrities bring a certain credibility and legitimacy in promoting brands and highlighting their philosophy. A celebrity endorsement can be considered a brand collaboration when the brand and the ambassador create products together or when the celebrity's image (personality, competencies, values, etc.) is staged in order to better highlight the brand's or the product's characteristics. However, the use of celebrities can be different according to the culture. While in US and Europe the product precedes the definition of the advertising campaign, the Japanese rely on the reputation of the celebrity or talent when designing an advertising campaign. Based on this approach, it has been discovered, over the years, that in Japan having a product endorsed by a celebrity may increase its exposure by up to 30% over a limited period. Taking into account these cultural differences, we identify two forms of partnerships between brands and celebrities (Table 3.1).

In this part, we consider a celebrity endorsement as a form of brand collaboration based on the idea that a celebrity can be perceived as a brand (Halonen-Knight and Hurmerinta, 2010).

Table 3.1 Brand collaborations with celebrities

Kinds of collaboration	*Definitions*	*Examples*
Co-branded products	Collaboration between a brand and a celebrity involving a co-creation and a co-naming of a new product	- Tommy Hilfiger & Gigi Hadid - Mont Blanc & Miles Davis - Adidas & Pharrell Williams
Brand ambassador	Collaboration between a brand and a celebrity staging in the communications messages	- Nespresso & George Clooney - Lidl & Heidi Klum - L'Oreal & Kristina Bazan - Levi's & Chiara Ferragni - Disney & Chiara Ferragni

3.1 WHEN BRANDS CREATE PRODUCTS WITH CELEBRITIES

Nowadays, celebrities are not only communication levers, they can also collaborate with brands to create products and to promote them on social media. Italian digital influencer, Chiara Ferragni, known for her lifestyle blog "The blond salad," has partnered with Shop Disney (2018) to create a limited-edition capsule collection of shoes, inspired by Minnie Mouse. This collaboration was strong and credible since the Italian influencer's posts frequently express her love for Disney. She often posts pictures showing the Mickey Mouse tattoo on her wrist, and most recently posted her newborn son in a Mickey Mouse Blanket. This kind of collaboration is very effective in selling Disney products and is described in a study showing that both brand attitudes and purchase intentions are positively influenced by the digital influencer's attractiveness and by the congruence between the digital influencer and the brand (Torres,

Augustos and Matos, in press). On the same principle, Tommy Hilfiger created a capsule collection with Gigi Hadid (2018) to design trendy city outfits that are a real success given the notoriety of the top model.

Creating a new product with a celebrity allows the telling of a story, like the Mont Blanc Great Characters Miles Davis Limited Edition pen (2017) which was created as a homage to the great American musician. The Limited Edition tells the story of Mile Davis through the elaborate pattern on the white gold cap. Each detail evokes the five major phases of American jazz led by Davis and then provides a product targeting fans of this music style.

In the music sector, Universal Music establishes contact between brands and singers in order to create musical events for specific occasions. For instance, for the launching of its new mobile phone, the Galaxy S6, Samsung organized a private showcase with the artist Mika, orchestrated by Universal Music and Brands and then broadcast on TV channels. In the same vein Givenchy, the famous French cosmetic brand, collaborated with the singer Jacob Banks, an English singer and songwriter, to produce the song for the launching of a new Givenchy perfume (2018).

Brand collaboration success depends upon the authenticity of the collaboration. This is the reason why Chopard, the luxury Swiss brand for watches and jewellery, unveiled Rihanna's love for Chopard jewellery to promote the capsule collection of jewellery designed by Rihanna. The press release highlighted this quote from Rihanna "I have always been in love with Chopard's exquisite jewellery, so to actually design collections with them is something I still can't believe." The love story between Rihanna and Chopard has been put to the forefront. Now, the duo has partnered to create a modern collection inspired by Rihanna's island roots – the lush gardens of Barbados and the electricity of Carnival.

Celebrities inspire brands and their artistic directors. For instance, the famous Hermès luxury bag, Birkin, comes from the meeting on a Paris-London flight in 1981 between Jane Birkin (a British actress and singer) and Jean Louis Dumas, president of Hermès. Jane Birkin explained to him the problem she had as a young mother: she could not find a handbag to store all her belongings and that of her baby daughter that was both practical and elegant. They started their collaboration and the Birkin bag of Hermès was born, with the name of its muse. The authenticity of this collaboration made, and still makes, sense and it creates value for consumers who purchase a bag that encapsulates the real life of women.

3.2 WHEN BRANDS USE CELEBRITIES TO PROMOTE THEIR PRODUCTS

Being well-known, endorsers are supposed to raise attention and interest and thus facilitate the awareness and the appropriation of the endorsed offer by the audience (Erfgen et al., 2015). Furthermore, the presence of a well-known figure creates an emotional link and generates a positive attitude towards the ad and the endorsed object (Knoll and Matthes, 2017, Dibble et al., 2016). The keys to the success of these partnerships between brands and celebrities are: 1) credibility, 2) attractiveness, 3) consistency, and 4) storytelling. When L'Oréal chose the ageless Jane Fonda to promote their anti-aging product range (2006), it was credible because Jane Fonda is a senior with a naturally less wrinkled skin. When Nespresso selected George Clooney to promote their premium coffee capsules and machines (2005), they wanted to transfer the actor's chic attractiveness to their high-range products. Again, when Tony Parker promoted French Quick fast food restaurants, it was consistent because Tony Parker, as both French and American, promotes the good taste of the hamburger.

Using celebrities in advertisements accelerates products sales. Marc Jacobs has always been aware of the power of celebrities. In his advertising campaigns, we can see the most famous celebrities promoting his creations. For instance, in the perfumes sector, Victoria Beckham, Dakota Fanning, Miley Cyrus, Sofia Coppola and Kaia Gerber embody the Daisy fragrance from Marc Jacobs.

Celebrities are helpful in convincing the audience. For example, in 2018 Zalando invited four celebrities– the German athlete Alexandra Wester, the French model Sonia Ben Ammar, the Belgian activist Hanne Gaby and also the American singer Beth Ditto – to display the unique character of women through their different strong personalities and to celebrate self-acceptance. The advertisement shows the four talents in their different environments, wearing their favourite pieces from the new collection. The presence of these four celebrities legitimates the campaign's slogan "Fashion without limits."

In the cosmetic market, celebrities can be particularly effective in humanizing a brand and eliciting empathy (Fleck, Michel and Zeitoun 2014). The ambassadors of L'Oréal are actresses such as Jane Fonda, Eva Longoria and Julianne Moore, top models such as Doutzen Kroes, Natasha Poly and Karlie Kloss, and singers such as Jennifer Lopez. The L'Oréal

Image 3.1 *Lacoste & Novak Djocovik*

Image 3.2 *Lacoste & Novak Djocovik*

Paris ambassadors all have extraordinary careers and each embodies, in their own way, a singular vision of beauty.

Many brands collaborate with sport celebrities in order to be associated to sporty values or to remember theirs roots. For instance, in 2018, Lacoste chose a new ambassador, the tennis player Novak Djokovic, the world number one, to celebrate and reinforce the origin of their founder Mr. Lacoste, who was himself a famous tennis player.

However, nowadays celebrities evolve. It has become more frequent to use CEOs, company founders or artistic directors as ambassadors to communicate expertise and authenticity to consumers (Fleck, Michel and Zeitoun, 2014). While regular celebrities can magically transport consumers to an idealized place, famous CEOs, company founders and artistic directors

CONSUMER TESTIMONY

Bettina, 55-years-old, married, three children, nurse, English, Shakira & Activia (interviewed in November 2018)

As long as I remember, I've always loved Shakira. She represents for me the ideal woman – she's beautiful, very active and seems so nice. I still listen to the songs she made like 15 years ago. For me, they're not aging and neither is she. I remember that Shakira was the only reason for me to see the Football World Cup in 2009; her song "This time for Africa" was amazing. As I love her so much, I want to be part of what she does. I saw her on the advertisement for those yogurts brand Activia. I immediately wanted to try it! I was used to my old Taillefine 0% yogurts but I was still overweight anyway. I thought to myself, Shakira did a commercial for this. Maybe I should try! Of course I did not believe in any magic but I was thinking, maybe that will take me closer to her somehow. I think I wouldn't have been so interested if it were presented by someone else. It's not like I was imagining anything but seeing her pretty face giving me some possibilities to change things in my life, I said to myself, "Why not?"

are perceived as aspirational models (Zeitoun, Michel and Fleck, in press). They are ordinary people with an extraordinary story – Steve Jobs (Apple), Richard Branson (Virgin) or Karl Lagerfeld (Chanel). Celebrities can also be ordinary people who have become influencers as they are genuinely perceived as "one of us." Today, the world of communication is changing. For instance, the new L'Oréal Paris ambassador is Kristina Bazan, a famous blogger, confirming the ever-stronger influence of celebrities from social media. While they are less exposed on classic media than actresses, singers or models, these influencers have a real community on which brands are now relying. Very active on social networks, these new celebrities have perfectly mastered the new codes of communication and have accessible personality traits that directly communicate with their Internet users. By joining the L'Oréal ambassadors' team, Kristina Bazan has confirmed the brand's commitment to Web 3.0 communication. This example is not unique – Chiara Farrangi is considered to be the most powerful blogger (The Blonde Salad) on the planet and has collaborated with leading luxury houses and magazines. With almost 8 million subscribers on Instagram, her blog has become a real business, attracting the biggest brands.

In an opposite way, from the beginning of Dove's brand story the company has used ordinary women to promote its products. Dove's purpose is to improve women's social representation, reinforcing the values of natural beauty and high self-esteem. Even if 100% of women agree with these values, they still need an aspirational model and an ideal to dream about. This is why even if the values of simplicity and sincerity are growing in our society, collaborations between brands and celebrities keep their relevance for consumers.

THE LEGISLATION AROUND INFLUENCE MARKETING

The use of influencers has become a real opportunity for brands. This practice is recent at the level of traditional advertising which explains why the laws that frame these practices are still underdeveloped. From 2010, when Instagram was created, until now, the practices that frame collaborations between brands and influencers have been unclear. Even if influencers have the ability to choose between hashtags such as #ad or #sp to warn their audience that it is a paid collaboration, the mandatory nature of this is uncertain. In the same way that brands buy advertising space, they now buy a showcase on the Instagram account of an influencer. The only difference is that on Instagram nothing forces brands and influencers to register the nature of their collaborations. This concerns Instagram and has pushed the company to develop new tools designed to bring more transparency. For example, the appearance of the "Paid partnership with" tag, created in February 2017 by the developers of Instagram, is becoming popular. It informs users that this is a paid-for collaboration. This new tag can be displayed not only on classic posts, but also on Instastories. For Instagram, putting in place a tool allowing the transparency of paid collaborations on the network is essential, especially for the 700 million daily users who trust them.

Source: www.tanke.fr/
marketing-dinfluence-et-collaboration-quelle-legislation/

The use of celebrities is not only reserved for selling products but also for promoting good causes. Non-profit organizations use ambassadors to solicit donations. For 17 years, the French Red Cross enjoyed the benefit of top model Adriana Karembeu as an endorser of the organization's values. The top model ambassador was always well motivated and committed to working with volunteers. In another context, football legend David Beckham supports UNICEF. In 2015, UNICEF and the former Manchester United football icon launched 7: The David Beckham UNICEF Fund to mark David's tenth year as a UNICEF Goodwill Ambassador. The 7 Fund is a unique partnership, with the goal of helping children around the world – especially girls – break down the barriers that too often steal dreams away: bullying, violence, child marriage, and missed education.

Celebrities who support NGOs highlight their personal values and it also helps them build their image. Surveys have demonstrated that celebrity endorsement creates equity for both the endorsed brand and the endorsing celebrity (Seno and Lukas, 2007).

TRANSCEND POTENTIAL MISCONCEPTIONS

- Collaborations with celebrities go beyond the simple status of brand ambassador.
- Collaborations with celebrities can bring value to consumers if they are authentic.
- Celebrity endorsements create equity for both the endorsed brand and the endorsing celebrity.

INTERVIEW WITH ADAM PETRICK
Global Director of Brand and Marketing, Puma, Boston, USA

"The first ever sneakers collaboration that achieved cult status among women"

Keywords: story doing

Actors: Puma, Rihanna

Puma is a multinational company that designs athletic and casual apparel and footwear. Its headquarters are in Bavaria, Germany. Puma is the third largest sportswear manufacturer in the world. The company was founded in 1948 and has been a public company since 1986. Nowadays the company employs more than 10,000 people worldwide and distributes its products in over 120 countries and in 2017 saw a €4.136 billion turnover.

Rihanna is a 30-year-old Barbadian singer, songwriter, actress, and businesswomen. Rihanna started her music career at the early age of 16 when she signed with Def Jam. Today, she has won multiple industry accolades including Grammys and MTV awards. Recognized as a pop icon of today's music, Rihanna is one of the best-selling music artists of all time, with 250 million records sold worldwide. In 2012, Forbes ranked her the fourth most powerful celebrity worldwide.

1) How was the collaboration announced?

In December 2014, it was confirmed that Rihanna would become the creative director of the fashion sportswear brand Puma, overseeing the brand's women's line which included collaborations in apparel and footwear. Rihanna released her first collaboration trainers in the fall of 2015. In 2016 and 2017, Rihanna debuted her clothing line with Puma at New York and Paris fashion week. The collection was met with rave reviews from fashion critics.

Overall, the collaboration was activated throughout a full 360° marketing and communication campaign, including ATL advertisings and BTL, POS advertisings, digital campaigns and PR coverage (interviews, PR clippings, etc.).

2) What were Puma's expectations for this collaboration?

Puma was initially looking for a female sports ambassador for Puma's Women's Training Category but it was hard to find a superstar athlete with international appeal. Puma decided to try something else and wondered who would meet its iconic brand values. That is when the choice of Rihanna was found. Like the brand, Rihanna is a risk taker; she does not necessarily follow the rules, is never satisfied, and she is always trying to do better. Furthermore, she has a broad crossover appeal (is followed by people who love street wear and high fashion) and we felt that she had the ability to make a big impact on the brand. Partnering with a personality like Rihanna, who meets the brand values and has crossover appeal, Puma was expecting an increase in sales through word of mouth; surprising its audience was seen as being more fashionable and premium.

3) What did this partnership bring to Rihanna?

For Rihanna, this collaboration was an honour in collaborating with a renowned premium brand and at the same time the collaboration served as a new challenge for her as she had to envision and create her own sneaker line. Rihanna's participation in the creative process of making a sneaker would benefit her as it would surprise her own fan base and earn royalties in a highly successful collaboration.

4) What were the fruits of the collaboration and what did it finally bring to Puma?

Puma was very impressed to have a personality so involved and creative. Rihanna completely changed the direction of women sneakers. Consequently, her creations influenced the design of many items in the Puma general collection.

In its financial report for the first quarter of 2017, Puma reported a net income increase of 92%. These results confirmed an upward trend that started soon after the start of the collaboration with Rihanna. Puma's share price was up $200 since the announcement of the partnership. Furthermore, in a sneaker culture which is fairly dominated by men, Rihanna is the first woman to receive the Shoe of the Year award from Football News – for the Fenty & Rihanna Creeper in 2016. She created the first ever sneakers collaboration to achieve cult status amongst women.

5) Who worked on this collaboration?

The global marketing team of Puma, based in Boston and directed by Adam Petrick, worked on this collaboration together with Rihanna and her styling team.

6) Overall, what were the best parts of the partnership?

Rihanna was very involved and creative which positively impressed all of the Puma team. The result of this collaboration was definitely one of the best parts. The critics were positive on all sectors – from buyers to fashion critics. Vogue Magazine stated "Fenty and Puma has kept one step ahead, so to speak, thanks in part to shoe designs that think outside the box."

7) What do you believe were the keys of success in this partnership?

Rihanna's motivation was a huge key to its success. From the very beginning, Rihanna had a very clear vision of what she wanted to achieve (in December, the contract was signed, in January, there was a meeting to discuss the product designs). Rihanna took part in the creative process: she suggested aesthetic guidelines and had a very clear vision of the range of models that she wanted to create.

Rihanna's first sneaker release sold out online within three hours of its pre-sale launch. Most importantly, listening and truly paying attention to the partner is essential. If you trust you've picked the right person, it does not matter what you have in mind; you should follow the heart and spirit of your partner. Partners should collaborate and listen to each other to make a successful partnership. For Puma, it's all about story telling through story doing.

INTERVIEW WITH GIANFRANCO BRUNETTI AND ISABELA LINK

Marketing Director – Head of brand & strategy and PR & Social media

Consultant marketing – International PR, Social media & Influencer marketing

"An unexpected collaboration was hard discounter Lidl's gateway into the fashion and beauty world"

Keywords: perfect fit

Actors: Lidl, Heidi Klum

Lidl is one of the leading discounter supermarket chains in the world, offering their customers quality products for the best price. With headquarters in Germany and over 10,000 stores worldwide, Lidl operates in over 27 European countries and the USA. It is the second biggest distributor group worldwide with a revenue of around €80 billion.

Heidi Klum was born in Germany in 1973, and lives in Los Angeles, USA. Heidi Klum is an actress, fashion designer, model, television personality, businesswoman, and television producer.

1) How did Lidl decide to announce the collaboration?

Lidl globally announced the partnership in June 2017. The whole communication around the launch collection was carefully orchestrated with an integrated 4-phased communication campaign:

1) 6 June – The announcement: a press release and one defined key visual were spread around the globe announcing that style icon Heidi Klum was teaming up with Lidl. No further details were revealed at that date.
2) 10 August – The global roll-out: the second key visual and first highlight pieces were shared with the media. From that day on, 140 influencers started their communications and spread the word about the collection.
3) 7 September – LETSWOW NYC – Lidl Fashion Event by Heidi Klum: the entire collection was presented to an international audience during New York Fashion Week to 340 guests, a mix of fashion editors, famous influencers and celebrities who were flown in from all over Europe and the USA. On top of that, the whole world was invited to tune in via Livestream.
4) 18 September – Sales started in over 10,000 stores.

2) What were Lidl's expectations for the partnership?

Lidl had successfully achieved being perceived as a provider of great products of great quality at a great price, but predominantly in the food division. Building on those achievements, Lidl set itself the objective of taking the next step and initiating this mind-set also for the non-food division of "textiles." Lidl wanted to offer its customers real fashion, not just textiles, at an affordable price. What many people didn't know is that the discounter is the eighth biggest textile retailer in Germany. Lidl has the expertise and resources. The challenge was, that, at that time, Lidl didn't have any kind of fashion credibility. This had to be changed.

To prove its expertise and relevance to the fashion market, Lidl needed an external supporter to underline its intentions in a credible way: Heidi Klum, a celebrity globally known for fashion, style, her German roots – Lidl's home market – and a down-to-earth attitude.

Lidl and Heidi pursued their unified mission of making fashion affordable for every woman ... with success.

3) What were the fruits of the collaboration and what did it finally bring to Lidl?

The Esmara by Heidi Klum collection includes five capsules, a great combination of essentials (jeans, shirts, etc.) with some highlight pieces – all available for a very accessible price of between €5 and €25.

Each capsule celebrates a dedicated overall topic, beginning with the first one #letswow, released last September, to #letscelebrate last December, #letsdenim in February, #Letslovesummer in June and finally #letsshakeitup, on sale in September. As well as their individual story angles, they all reflect and represent the core Lidl value of "joy of life."

Thanks to the fully integrated campaign around the hashtag #letswow (PR, TV, digital, social media, influencer, events, and POS) Lidl not only successfully widened its target groups, but also achieved its aim being perceived as a serious fashion retailer. The Esmara by Heidi Klum brand has been mentioned in renowned fashion and lifestyle magazines alongside some of the world's most exclusive fashion labels and has been recognized by international fashion influencers. That was a great success.

Just to give you some numbers for the first collection:

- We achieved a total media value of around €90 million.
- 140 influencers reached around 343 million people.
- 20 million people tuned in via Livestream (Europa and USA).
- And last, but not least, we registered a drastic increase in social media sign ups with a reach of 12 million views.

4) Who worked on this collaboration?

Three internal teams have been involved in the collaboration: Project management; Purchasing department; and Communications/PR. These teams were in steady exchange with Heidi Klum and her team to discuss the collections, marketing and communications.

5) Overall, what were the best parts of the partnership?

The best part was the unexpected great success of the partnership with a media value of around €90 million for the first launch, ten times more than for a regular collection launch. For the first time, Lidl has played a role in the international fashion industry. That is really something Lidl could never have dreamed of! Heidi's partnership affected the entire company as well as the brand equity!

6) And the more difficult parts of the partnership?

The partnership went very well. It was a pleasure to work with Heidi and her team. We are now looking forward to the next fashion adventure.

7) What do you believe were the keys of success of this partnership?

- Above all – a winning duo. This partnership with Heidi Klum was a huge success as she perfectly represents and complements the Lidl values and actively participated in the whole design and communication process.
- Our fully integrated 360° communication strategy around the hashtag #letswow –
- including influencers, PR, events digital and social media but also TV, OOH, print and POS marketing.
- A very strong and effective launch campaign with the kick-off event during NYC Fashion Week, which positioned Lidl as a confident and serious actor on the global fashion scene. NYFW constitutes the ideal platform to generate relevant global content, global awareness and reach and, above all, fashion credibility. It was the first time a discounter had presented a collection during this event.
- Achieving global awareness while remaining locally relevant through a successful mix of central and local communications, as well as global and local influencers.
- To sum up, it has been a very well developed mixture of all of the factors mentioned above that finally led to the success and spread the

word that Lidl and Heidi are making fashion affordable for everyone. Fashion should be fun and everybody should be able to afford this pleasure.

8) What parts of the partnership could have been improved?

The whole collaboration was a great success. The only thing I could think of that could have been improved is the time lapse in between the collections: three months might have been too short.

LINKS

#letswow www.youtube.com/watch?v=p6rfjwhgMvY

#letscelebrate www.youtube.com/watch?v=Lup9e8d8CPw

#Letsdenim www.youtube.com/watch?v=D1bNNlsh14E

#letslovesummer www.youtube.com/watch?v=_vD8FR9uBXw

Image 3.3 *Lidl & Heidi Klum*

Image 3.4 *Lidl & Heidi Klum*

Image 3.5 *Lidl & Heidi Klum*

REFERENCES

Dibble, J.L., Hartmann, T. and Rosaen, S.F. (2016). Parasocial interaction and parasocial relationship: conceptual clarification and a critical assessment of measure. *Human Communication Research, 42*(1), 21–44.

Erfgen, C., Zenker, S. and Sattler, H. (2015). The vampire effect: When do celebrity endorsers harm brand recall? *International Journal of Research in Marketing, 32*(2), 155–163

Fleck, N., Michel, G. and Zeitoun, V. (2014). Brand personification through the use of spokespeople: An exploratory study of ordinary employees, CEOs, and celebrities featured in advertising. *Psychology & Marketing, 31*(1), 84–92.

Knoll, J. and Matthes, J. (2017). The effectiveness of celebrity endorsements: a meta-analysis. *Journal of the Academy of Marketing Science, 45*(1), 55–75.

Halonen-Knight, E. and Hurmerinta, L. (2010). Who endorses whom? Meanings transfer in celebrity endorsements. *Journal of Product and Brand Management, 19*(6), 452–460.

Seno, D. and Lukas, B.A. (2007). The equity effect of product endorsement by celebrities: A conceptual framework from a co-branding perspective. *European Journal of Marketing, 41*(1/2), 121–134.

Torres, P., Augusto, M., & Matos, M. (2019). Antecedents and outcomes of digital influencer endorsement: An exploratory study. Psychology & Marketing, 36(12), 1267–1276.

Zeitoun, V., Michel, G. and Fleck, N. (2020). When brands use CEOs and employees as spokespersons: A framework for understanding internal endorsement. *Qualitative Market Research* (in press).

CHAPTER 4

Brand collaborations with cultural organizations

Brands do not only collaborate with brands, artists and celebrities, they can also team up with cultural institutions. In this case, brands are looking for cultural recognition within society. A brand collaboration with a cultural organization means that a brand partners with a cultural institution such as a museum, cultural centre, theatre, opera, etc. In the same vein as collaborations with artists, an association with a cultural organization allows brands to penetrate the art world. The collaboration between a brand and a cultural organization can take different forms such as the launch of a new product, the creation of an event or a cross-sales promotion (Table 4.1).

Table 4.1 Brand collaborations with cultural organizations

Kinds of collaboration	Definitions	Examples
Co-branded products	Collaboration between a brand and a cultural institution involving the co-creation and a co-naming of a new product	- Vans & Van Gogh museum - Uniqlo & MoMA
Co-branded experiences	Collaboration between a brand and a cultural organization involving the creation of a common experience	- Jean-Paul Gaultier & Grand Palais - Bic & Musée 104 - Honest & We Love Green Festival

(Continued)

Kinds of collaboration	Definitions	Examples
Cross-sales promotions	Collaboration between a brand and a cultural organization involving the creation of a common sales promotion	- Hotel Park Hyatt & MoMA - Bank of America & U.S. Museums

4.1 WHEN BRANDS CREATE PRODUCTS WITH CULTURAL ORGANIZATIONS

Brands that collaborate with museums frequently launch new products inspired by this collaboration. In 2018, the French watch brand Aight partnered with the Museum Pompidou in Paris launching three watch models in honour of three artists from the French Museum. The watch dials incorporate Mondrian's (a French painter) primary color lines, Pollock's paint chips (an American painter) and concentric Kupka (a Czech painter) shapes. This collaboration takes advantage of the renown of the museum and its artists and it also allows the museum to bring art out into the street. In the same vein, Uniqlo, as multi-year sponsor of the New York Museum of Modern Art (MoMA), launched SPRZ NY (Surprize New York). Under SPRZ NY, Uniqlo put artworks inspired by top contemporary artists such as Andy Warhol (an American artist), Jean-Michel Basquiat (an American painter), and Keith Haring (an American artist) on some 200 products. Some of the artists, including Ryan McGinness (an American painter), will personally design clothing items based on the work displayed in MoMA. The Uniqlo/MoMA partnership works in so many dimensions (Aaker, 2013). It adds value to products by creating energy and interest in Uniqlo's clothing designs and allows the close association of Uniqlo and MoMA to be more visible. This partnership not only enhances the MoMA and Uniqlo brands, but also creates an innovative and personalized experience for shoppers and museum visitors alike. Even though Uniqlo and MoMA both operate in different fields, they both aim to promote art as widely as possible.

In the same spirit, the Van Gogh Museum in Amsterdam and the Vans shoes brand led an unusual collaboration for the artist's fans. This partnership gave birth to a collection of shoes and clothing (sneakers, caps, etc.) with motifs inspired by the work of the painter including his famous Self Portrait (1889) and The Sunflowers (1888). These items represent unique pieces and a portion of the profits from sales will be donated to the museum.

Image 4.1 *Van Gogh Museum & Vans*

Image 4.2 *Van Gogh Museum & Vans*

CONSUMER TESTIMONY

Kate, 37-years-old, English, seller at London airport, Johnnie Walker & Game of Thrones (interviewed in November 2018)

For us it's an event to sell new products. This collaboration is, I think, very different from what we are used to see. As Johnnie Walker is a great whisky company, we wouldn't expect them to create a product with a TV show, especially Game of Thrones. I believe this goes far beyond just communication because the product itself is totally disruptive! Whisky is usually drunk at ambient temperature, it shouldn't be too warm or too cold, otherwise it loses its taste. It's very specific. This product is different, it's meant to be drunk ice cold. The image of Game of Thrones, with the White Walkers coming from the North, the cold country, is very credible. They played with both the name of the host brand Johnnie Walker and the White Walkers, and the cold and freezing ambiance of the show. As for me, as a seller, I have to say that it is a real change from our traditional products and we see new customers that are curious about it. Young people are keen on ice-cold cocktails, that's why we also provide a few recipes. As a seller of alcohol, of course I enjoy a good whisky, and I have to say that this one is a good one!

4.2 WHEN BRANDS SUPPORT AND EXHIBIT IN MUSEUMS, FESTIVALS, AND OPERAS

B rands collaborating with cultural institutions look for a new experience which will create a unique event for consumers and citizens. This was the case when Dior collaborated with the Museum d'Arts Décoratifs (MAD) : "Christian Dior, designer of dreams" was an exceptional retrospective, organized by the Museum of Decorative Art (MAD) with the support of the Christian Dior house on the occasion of the 70th anniversary of the brand. Thousands of documents and a hundred works of art dedicated to the inventor of the "New Look" were collected in an area of 3,000m^2. This exhibition had a record attendance for the museum with more than 450,000 visitors in five months, from all social backgrounds and cultural horizons. The success can be explained by the attractiveness of a mythical fashion house, Christian Dior, and an extraordinary historical content. Social networks were also an asset in creating an incredible international buzz around this event. This partnership brought an improved image for both partners.

In the same vein, The Grand Palais has welcomed Hermès, introducing the poetic and flamboyant universe of Leila Menchari (Tunisian designer). Even if the Hermès house does not consider this exhibition a collaboration with The Grand Palais, the choice of this venue is totally consistent with Hermès' interest in the world of horses. Hermès organizes a horse show jumping competition in the centre of the Grand Palais museum, involving the greatest riders in the world. This event, open to the public is a meeting place for the horse riding world with a series of displays including an equestrian show. This is an opportunity for spectators to experience unique moments and to recall the origins of the luxury brand. The Grand Palais has also opened its doors to the creator Jean-Paul Gaultier by exhibiting original pieces of the stylist created between 1970 and 2013. This retrospective, accompanied by archives, stage costumes, film clips, parades, concerts music videos, dance and television have once again attracted a large audience to reinforce the aura of the brand. This successful

Image 4.3 *Grand Palais & Jean-Paul Gauthier*

collaboration shows the growing interest of people in the fashion world and suggests museums are evolving and opening up to brand collaboration.

Exhibitions devoted to brands are becoming more frequent, and concentrate on luxury brands: Dior at MAD (450,000 visitors in 2017), Bulgari at The Grand Palais (120,000 visitors in 2011), and Yves Saint Laurent at The Petit Palais (250,000 visitors in 2010). Why such interest? In the world of luxury, these collaborations correspond with the new expectations of consumers who are looking for meaning. These exhibitions highlight the heritage of brands and integrate them into the art world. But it is not enough that brands decide to make exhibitions to promote themselves; visitors are not fooled and look for authenticity and significance. Chanel's exhibition for N°5 at the Palais de Tokyo was disappointing, from the visitors' point of view, because it was seen as a showcase for the brand with no historical research. Brand exhibitions must go beyond the mere advertisement process and presuppose collaboration between a brand and a curator of exhibitions in order to transfer into the world of art.

Luxury brands are not the only ones collaborating with museums. For instance, the founders of the international brand Bic decided to exhibit their art collection at the modern art museum Musée 104 in Paris. Bic is a world leader in the areas of writing, lighters, and razors, and showed, for the first time, its contemporary art collection initiated by Marcel Bich, founder of the company. Objects that are accessible to all, Bic products have inspired many artists.

This exhibition, in partnership with Musée 104, brings together more than 140 works from around the world, inspired by Bic products. The exhibition shows how the brand is a source of inspiration for artists such as Alberto Giacomettit (a Swiss painter) or Rene Magritte (a Belgian painter), through Fernand Lege (a French painter) or Alighiero Boett (an Italian painter). The Bic collection exhibition is a way to share with the public unpublished art works that reflect the strength of the brand in society. This partnership between Bic and the art museum is the proof of the fine frontier between both spheres. The Musée 104 (Paris) and Bic share a common vision: touch and inspire as many people as possible. Completely free, with a clear, simple and immersive scenography the exhibition is intended for all audiences.

Image 4.4 *Bic & museum gallery 104*

Although luxury brands are the most usual brands for collaborations between brands and museums, the artistic laboratory of the Bel brand (Lab'Bel), the Bic exhibition and the recent exhibition at MoMA "Streetwear that changed the world" show that collaborations between brands and cultural organizations can also involve popular brands. Indeed, the exhibition in MoMA shows more than 150 brands from Supreme,

Champion, and Adidas, to Converse and other iconic lifestyle brands. The goal of this exhibition is to highlight the important influence of these brands on culture and modern design. In the exhibition, Issey Miyake, Ralph Lauren, and Rick Owens are among ten designers collaborating with the Museum of Modern Art's (MoMA) Design Store on a range of products in the upcoming exhibition "Items: Is Fashion Modern?." This partnership is a collaborative work where the museum wants to integrate the history and the current role of brands in the world. Mary Katrantzou (a Greek fashion designer) and Marni (a luxury Italian fashion brand) are also among the brands that influence the fashion world with the black turtleneck, the Breton shirt, Ray Ban aviators, and the Champion hoodie. Thanks to these partnerships with MoMA, the brands have become iconic; at the same time this event represents an evolution of the museum from the first fashion exhibition in 1944.

Collaborations between brands and museums benefit both parties. Brands benefit from the aura of museums and the art world and museums integrate themselves into the world of events. This is the case of the exhibition devoted to the Cartier brand "Cartier: style and history" at The Grand Palais (Paris). The curator from the museum set up the entire exhibition and has prevented the brand exhibition from being perceived as disguised advertising.

These collaborations between brands and museums show how brands can be accepted as heritage objects. By using the heritage within a museum, brands no longer rely just on the logic of the market– the brand becomes a sacred and inalienable common good (Chaney, Pulh and Mencarelli, 2018).

In the entertainment sector, brands support also festivals and concerts. For instance, Absolut has partnered with Little Sun (the Foundation of Olafur Eliasson) to transform the festival experience at the Coachella Valley Music and Arts Festival. Absolut created an interactive art bar designed by Little Sun and situated in the Coachella Festival – the goal was to bring a more positive social ambiance through art and cocktails.

In the same vein of unveiling one facet of its identity, in 2018 Shiseido supported the exhibition "A Forest where Gods Live Art," devised by teamlab and based on the concept "Nature Becomes Art." The exhibition took place in Japan (Mifuneyama Rakuen) with 14 main exhibits, where the Waso tea house presented the concept of Waso, the new brand of Shiseido skincare. The visitors could then explore the world of Waso through the "five senses." This collaboration meets Shiseido's goals, launching a new Waso skincare line targetting millennials in the USA and Asian countries with the concept of "Feel beautiful in your own skin with skincare that respects the uniqueness and the flavour of nature."

Again in the context of a music festival, the Honest drink brand joined the We Love Green Festival and welcomed people to its stand to taste its new range of eco-friendly ice tea and herbal tea. This collaboration between Honest and the We Love Green Festival made sense to people because both partners espouse socially responsible values and want to show that eco-friendly products and good drinks can be accessible at a music festival.

4.3 WHEN BRANDS AND CULTURAL ORGANIZATIONS PROVIDE CROSS-SALES PROMOTIONS

Cross sales promotions with cultural institutions are increasing. For instance, the hotel Park Hyatt in New York collaborates with MoMA to provide a unique value to their clients. With the anticipated openings of Park Hyatt, New York and Park Hyatt, Vienna, the hotel brand offered them special MoMA packages, providing exclusive access to the museum during their stay at the hotel. This cross-sales promotion attracted those interested in luxury hospitality and in the contemporary art of the prestigious institution.

It is also frequent to see banks collaborating with cultural organizations in order to offer their clients the opportunity to visit exhibition for free. For instance, the Bank of America offers cardholders the opportunity to visit more than 200 museums free of charge through its "Museums on Us" programme. These collaborations with different cultural organizations (for example, The Whitney Museum of American Art, The Metropolitan Museum of Art and the Staten Island Museum, Houston Zoo, etc.) allow the bank to provide learning experiences to its clients and to build strong relationships with them. On the other hand, the cultural organizations benefit from an increase in the numbers of visitors the collaboration attracts.

Overall, openness to the experience of art enhances individuals' creativity by imbuing them with a sense of inspiration (Carlucci and Schiuma, 2018). In particular, several studies have shown that individuals with open attitudes toward aesthetic experiences are more likely to be inspired, and therefore better able to generate creative solutions. The power of art appreciation, extended to a business environment, has also enhanced people's performance in product design, brand-naming, and problem solution generation (An and Youn, 2017).

TRANSCEND POTENTIAL MISCONCEPTIONS

- Brands' exhibitions with museums allow brands to enter the art world, which represents an amazing dream for companies who desire to be known not just as business actors but also as actors in the art world.
- Brand's exhibitions within cultural organizations increase brands' credibility and legitimacy.
- The authenticity of the partnership is a key to the brand collaboration's success.

INTERVIEW WITH CHAY COSTELLO
Associate Director of Merchandising at MoMA Design Store

"How to reflect and support a cultural exhibition through limited editions?"

Keywords: product drop, extend the museum exhibition experience, push the exhibition outside the museum

Actors: MoMA's exhibition "Items: Is Fashion Modern?"

MoMA, the Museum of Modern Art, is an art museum located in Midtown Manhattan in New York City, USA. MoMA is the largest museum of modern art in the US and is identified as one of the most influential museums of modern art in the world. It was established in 1929 and includes various area of art such as architecture, drawing, painting, sculpture, photography, etc. MoMA's collection contains over 200,000 works of modern and contemporary art. The museum has about 3 million visitors per year. It was in 1932 that MoMA established the world's first curatorial department devoted to architecture and design.

"Items: Is Fashion Modern" is an exhibition dedicated to historical fashion staples. This exhibition hosted a curated selection of garments and accessories that explore design in three areas: prototype, archetype, and stereotype. The exhibition explored the present, past and future of 111 clothing items and accessories that have had a strong influence in the twentieth and twenty-first centuries. Clothes are a way to document history, a way to understand society and technology. Clothing is both a means of production and supply but also a means of expressing individualism. The exhibition took place for four months from 1 October 2017 to 28 January 2018.

MoMA has major corporate partners such as Uniqlo, Target, and Volkswagen.

1) How was the collaboration announced?

Historically, the museum has chosen not to engage with fashion in its galleries. Therefore, MoMA hasn't had a fashion collection since the 1944.

In developing a suite of products inspired by the exhibition, we invested time into analyzing what type of audience we would be attracting. We wanted to attract an audience interested in iconic design. We had a lot of different ideas and ended up working with eleven different brands. The list included New Era (Yankees cap), Armor Lux for cotton T-shirt, Ray-Ban for their aviator sunglasses, Champion for a hoodie, Ralph Lauren for a polo, Issey Miyake for a knit shirt, Nike Sneakers designed by Virgil Abloh, silk scarves from Mary Katrantzou, Rick Owens and Francesco Risso of Marni. The collaborations with the brands were limited edition and were only available for the four months that the exhibition was on.

One of our special editions included a collaboration between Nike and Virgil Abloh, the designer of the iconic brand "Off-White" and current artistic director of Louis Vuitton men's wear collection since March 2018. For this collaboration we did what we call a product "drop." A product "drop" is a controlled release of a new product that's far faster than the traditional fashion cycle. We spread the message of this drop, "Nike Air Force 1," on social media and on MoMA's newsletter. Everything got sold out in less than a day! We set up our email and Instagram post at 6 a.m. and within 15 minutes we had hundreds of people standing outside to purchase the item. We had to shut down the sale and relocate it within just one hour due to the surplus of people desperate to purchase this co-branded product. When selling the product, we limited the sales to one pair per customer. Each purchase included a pair of custom socks and complimentary admission to MoMA.

In NYC and in big cities in general, the concept of a product drop associated with a personality or celebrity is becoming increasingly attractive to customers.

2) What were MoMA's expectations from this collaboration?

From these collaborations, we were able to draw a new audience to the museum. We also hoped that through these collaborations, our customers would remember their experience at MoMA every time they wore the product that they purchased at MoMA Design Store.

3) What did this partnership bring to the brands you collaborated with?

When we contacted brands such as Nike and Swatch, they were really enthusiastic and interested in partnering during the exhibition. To them, it was a celebration of their brand's being showcased in the museum and they embraced this opportunity to create limited editions products in collaboration with MoMA Design Store.

4) What were the fruits of the collaboration and what did it finally bring to MoMA?

Overall, the Nike sneakers, the New Era Yankees cap, the Champion hoodie, and the Breton shirt were on the top of our list. But the Nike Air Force 1 & Off-White by Virgil Abloh sold out within a day while the other four were available throughout the duration of the exhibition. So, the Nike sneakers were definitely a phenomenon! For each item, I would say the best-selling ones sold thousands and the less selling products sold hundreds.

5) Who worked on this collaboration?

The 11 brands worked with their designer directly. Some of the pieces like the New Era cap or the Swatch watches were directly from the exhibition. Meanwhile, other pieces like the Breton shirt or the scarfs based their products on the other iconic and classic designs portrayed in the exhibition.

6) Overall, what were the best parts of the partnership?

Everybody we worked with was very enthusiastic and really supportive and that is definitely the best part. This merchandise was very unique because we merchandise around nearly every exhibition to a larger or smaller degree but the merchandise around this exhibition was exceptional. Bringing back a fashion exhibition to MoMA after 40 years was an amazing experience.

7) And the more difficult parts of the partnership?

The hardest part was probably the beginning. We had so many ideas and brands interested it was hard to edit the list.

8) What do you believe were the keys of success of this partnership?

I believe that if you are going to work on a partnership, you really have to do the research to have a "win win" for both parties and find what you have in common and how you could support each other. On the other hand, if you have too many things in common, there could be a sense of predictability. Overall, a key to a successful collaboration is to have some common DNA but still be different enough to yield a surprising result.

9) What parts of the partnership could have been improved?

We could have made an improvement with our inventory levels. We didn't know how much of each item we would sell but, for example, we immediately sold all our baseball caps, Champion hoodies, and Breton shirts. Hence, we had to work very fast and be in a rush as the exhibition was four months and we had to get stock back as quickly as possible.

REFERENCES

Aaker, David (2013). Available online at www.prophet.com/2015/07/241-the-uniqlo-and-moma-a-partnership-that-wins/

An, D. and Youn, N. (2018). The inspirational power of arts on creativity. *Journal of Business Research*, 85, 467–475.

Carlucci, D. and Schiuma, G. (2018). An introduction to the special issue "The arts as sources of value creation for business: Theory, research, and practice." *Journal of Business Research*, 85, 337–341.

Chaney, D., Pulh, M. and Mencarelli, R. (2018). When the arts inspire businesses: Museums as a heritage redefinition tool of brands. *Journal of Business Research*, 85, 452–458.

CHAPTER 5

Brand collaborations with sports organizations

B rands also collaborate with sport organizations. In this case, brands are looking for values referring to the sport such as perseverance and competition and for a high recognition in the public society. Collaboration between BRANDS and sport organizations means that a brand collaborates with partners such as sport teams, stadiums, athletic events, etc. For a long time, brands have supported sport teams in different sectors through sponsorship. In this chapter, we shall analyze collaborations between brands and sport organizations involving four main forms: co-branded products, co-branded communications or events, cross-sales promotions and the naming of stadiums or sport events (see Table 5.1).

Sponsorship can be considered as a form of brand collaboration (Blackett, 2008). Sports sponsorship is financial or material support provided to an event, a federation, a sports team, or an athlete by an advertising partner in exchange for different forms of visibility and collaboration. The brand using sports sponsorship most often wants to take advantage of the visibility of the event or athletes in terms of media exposure. It is also the opportunity for a brand to be associated with values of adventure, humility, perseverance, and innovation. Usually, we distinguish three main forms of sports sponsorship:

- "Jersey sponsorship": The use of the athlete's jersey as an advertising space. Rakuten (a Japanese e-commerce group) sponsors FC Barcelona football team and appears on the jersey as the main sponsor of the Spanish team.

Table 5.1 Brand collaborations with sports organizations

Kinds of collaboration	Definition	Examples
Co-branded communication	Collaboration between a brand and a sport organization involving the co-creation of communication messages	- Adidas & Fifa World Cup - Coca-Cola & Fifa World Cup
Cross-sales promotion	Collaboration between a brand and a sport organization involving the creation of a common sales promotion	- McDonald's & PSG - Nivea & PSG
Naming	Collaboration between a brand and a sport organization involving the use of the brand name as the name of a competition or a stadium, etc.	Stadium names: - Allianz Arena (FC Bayern); - Groupama Stadium with a name of French insurance firm Sport events: - Monte Carlo Rolex Master (tennis) - Red Bull (F1), - Team Sky (cycling)
Co-branded products	Collaboration between a brand and an athlete or a sport organization involving both the co-creation and the co-naming of a new product	- Levi's & PSG - Lacoste & Roland Garros - Nike & Jordan

- "Official Supplier" or "Technical Partner": These designations make it possible to associate a brand with a team or a federation and to make this collaboration visible on stadium signs and in the media. Uniqlo provides Roger Federer with tennis wear.

- "Naming" is the fact of attaching the brand name to a competition or a stadium. The home ground of the Golden State Warriors Basketball team is called the Oracle Arena, taking its name from the US-based computer technology firm.

Beyond these three partnerships, we see more and more sport sponsorship deals integrating the creation of product ranges and cross-sales promotions. The reasons why companies undertake sponsorship activity in the sports sector are various. On the one hand, there is the communication aspect linked to the image and to the reputation of the company. On the other hand, there are the commercial factors related to the sale of products. And finally, sports sponsorship helps strengthen the corporate culture by playing on human relations. Collaboration between brands and sports organization therefore offers many opportunities for all types of companies (hospitality sector, BtoB, etc.), from visibility to strengthening internal cohesion.

5.1 WHEN BRANDS SUPPORT SPORTS ACTIVITIES

In the case of a sporting event, the brand seeks visibility that is generally obtained through advertising media during the event. For instance, Coca-Cola has partnered with many of the biggest sporting events since 1928. This presence of the brand alongside the greatest sportsmen of the world brings public awareness of it and a very positive image around the values of sharing and the joy provoked by these world events. For a team or an athlete, it is often the clothing and accessories that will serve as a means of visibility for the brand during broadcasts or press releases of the event. The visibility component of a sponsorship agreement is most often completed by various elements integrated in a global agreement:

- the availability of boxes or VIP tickets offered to partners or clients of the sponsor
- athlete or team participation in corporate events for external and internal audiences
- the participation of the athlete or the team in advertising campaigns

- the use of the sponsor title of the event or the sportsman in communications (promotions, advertising).

In the context of sports sponsorship, the brand seeks to benefit from image effects based on the values associated with the sport, the team or the athlete benefiting from the sponsorship action. For instance, football is linked to a popular image and aims at a very large population – it attracts the brands that target such audiences. Using this logic, Carrefour (a French retailer brand) has partnered the French football team since 1998. Carrefour is also part of the Tour de France (a French national multi-day bicycle stage race) with Vittel (water from the Nestlé group) and Skoda (a German brand car). This partnership makes it possible to relay this event in stores and to ensure a presence in the Tour caravan, which reaches 12 million spectators along the roads, and on the iconic white with red polka dot jersey of the best climber. In the same vein, because Wimbledon and ice cream make a perfect combination, Häagen-Dazs entered a partnership with the championships in 2016, offering ice

Image 5.1 *Häagen Dazs & Wimbledon*

cream during the tennis competition and creating a large campaign to support the Wimbledon event.

It is not possible to talk about brand collaboration in sports without mentioning the partnership between GoPro and Red Bull. GoPro (commercial action cameras) teams up with Red Bull not to promote its energy drinks but to collaborate in the creation of Red Bull sports events. Indeed, the Red Bull brand has become directly linked in consumers' minds with helping athletes to succeed in extreme sport. This has involved an enormous sports sponsorship strategy. As for the GoPro brand, beyond the product, it promotes the lifestyle of heroes every day. The two brands therefore collaborate on many events, the most emblematic of them being Felix Baumgartner (the Austrian skydiver) who jumped from the stratosphere in 2012, while being filmed by 35 cameras including GoPros. GoPro camera technology is the perfect complement to the sports events organized by Red Bull, offering athletes unprecedented opportunities.

Image 5.2 *Häagen Dazs & Wimbledon*

Image 5.3 *Redbull & GoPro*

Image 5.4 *Redbull & GoPro*

Sports sponsorship is also used and relayed internally for the cohesion and motivation of employees. Indeed, sports events are understood as tools to create a social identity around sports activities (Pierre and Tribou, 2013). For companies looking for both performance and significance for employees, sport represents a rich reservoir of symbols. Sports values provide a framework in which companies can anchor their vocabulary and techniques of training and development. The cohesion of the French Football Team was key to their success in the 2018 Football World Cup and is becoming a source of inspiration for management in companies.

The role of event communication in internal motivation and social cohesion is well known (Burlot and Pichot, 2004), including the sense of pride felt by staff following an event sponsored by their business. In this virtuous circle, SMA, a leading insurance company in the construction sector, has been working with skipper Paul Meilhat for four years in the framework of the Transat Jacques Vabre and thus promotes the social cohesion of employees who participate during the year in preparation for the sporting event.

The partnership between a brand and a sport team is a relevant to redefining brand identity, discursively repositioning the brand and building brand equity. A study concerning the collaboration between Adidas and the All Blacks Rugby team suggests the importance of an articulated campaign in order to increase the equity of corporate brands. Successful collaboration supposes the alignment of brand values, the collaboration between partners in terms of marketing communication and network of relationships (Motion, Leitch and Brodie 2003).

Social media activities are also important for the success of brand collaborations with sports organizations. A study by Do, Ko and Woodside (2015) showed that brand's sports sponsorship in social-media activities positively influences brand relationship quality. In particular, consumers, who have previously purchased products and services associated with a sports brand, perceive its sponsorship activities more positively in social media, compared to those consumers having no previous purchases of the sponsored brand. It seems that social media activities about a brand's sports sponsorship are more effective for brand customers than for non-customers.

5.2 WHEN BRANDS BECOME A NAME FOR SPORTS TEAMS, PLACES, COMPETITIONS

In the field of sports sponsorship, naming is the practice of giving a sports venue (a stadium), a competition or a sports team the name of a brand. The sponsor's logo is also most often associated with the new visual identity of the stadium or competition.

In the American basketball league, there are 30 grounds. Of these 30 grounds, 29 are named after a brand or company. Only Madison Square Garden in New York still resists the practice. These sponsors include American Airlines which gives its name to two venues: the American Airlines Arena in Miami and the American Airlines Center in Dallas. American Airlines has invested $42 million over 20 years to give its name to the Miami stadium and $195 million over 30 years for the Dallas stadium. Return on investment for brands is important – for every match, they enjoy considerable visibility at each event. In the NBA, there are also the AT&T Center in San Antonio, the Barclays Center in Brooklyn, the Oracle Arena for Golden State, the Pepsi Center in Denver, and the Toyota Center in Houston. Stadium naming has been in existence for more than 20 years in the United States and is used by all NBA franchises as they need this cash to grow and be competitive. In Europe, Bayern Munich and Arsenal were among the first clubs to choose the naming strategy by opening the Allianz Arena and the Emirates Stadium. These partnerships bring colossal sums to the clubs and a visibility and an international image to the brands.

Unlike the simple jersey sponsorship, which offers more or less space on the tunic of the sportsmen, the naming of the competitions presents the possibility of linking a name to that of a competition, so that it is quoted many times. Lidl (the German retailer) offered the right to attach their name to a competition. The German company chose the handball championship, and renamed it "Lidl Starligue." The German brand was approached by the world of football and rugby, but preferred to associate with a developing sport where the star system is less important. Such an approach enriches the values of the company and the brand image of the sport experience. The brand intends to generate traffic in stores and on the internet with, among other things, games to gain seats and signing sessions with handball teams.

Beyond the communication and the visibility of the brand sponsors, brands collaborate with sport organizations to launch new products. We shall develop this theme in the next section.

5.3 WHEN BRANDS CREATE PRODUCTS WITH AN ATHLETE OR SPORTS ORGANIZATION

The extraordinary partnership between the athletic shoe manufacturer Nike and the basketball legend Michael Jordan is arguably the most successful example of brand collaboration in history. From the beginning of the collaboration until now, Nike has released 50 shoes in the Jordan line. Now, Nike has created a subsidiary that produces Air Jordan products on which even the comma logo no longer appears. The myth goes beyond the man and the Air Jordan brand – Nike and Michael Jordan is an example of success for both partners and for consumers who buy highly technical products with a strong symbolic connection.

The football club, Paris Saint-Germain (PSG), has signed a partnership with the clothing brand, Levi's. They have joined forces to launch a clothing collection that combines authenticity and aesthetics. Thus, the Trucker jacket, a well-known model of Levi's has undergone some changes, playing with the image of Paris. On its left sleeve the jacket displays the logo of PSG and the name of the club is on the back. For PSG, it is about bringing passion into the daily lives of fans and makes this club a real community – not only around football, but also around a lifestyle. The PSG brand has become more international and more premium. For its part, Levi's has shown a passion for the city of Paris and the values of sport.

Image 5.5 *Nike & Jordan & PSG*

PSG collaborates also with the brand Nivea Men. Beyond the visibility of the cosmetics brand during PSG games, Nivea Men has launched limited-edition collector products. Hence Nivea Men provides personalized shower gels in the colours of PSG with famous footballer's names such as Zlatan Ibrahimovic, Edinson Cavani, Blaise Matuidi, David Luiz, or Salvatore Sirigu. It's a good way to boost Nivea Men's sales and bring a product in daily use to PSG fans.

Through collaborating with a major football club in Paris, Nivea wants to attract male clients. The aim of this partnership for Beiersdorf (Nivea's company owner) is to gain 1 million more consumers over three years. To achieve its objectives, Nivea offered a new advertising campaign utilizing

PSG players: David Luiz, Blaise Matuidi, Lucas, and Javier Pastore. In the first year, Nivea Men attracted 700,000 new customers, well beyond its expectations. Nivea's partnership with the Paris football club allowed its men's range to move from third place to second place in sales, after Mennen of L'Oreal. This partnership with the Parisian football club has worked well because PSG and Nivea Men are two brands with different images, but which share some common values. They are responsible, socially aware, and, above all, conquerors.

Roland-Garros and Lacoste is the story of a meeting between sport and French elegance. The historical partner of the French Open since 1971, each year the crocodile brand unveils new collections combining the tennis world and the elegance of the Lacoste brand. This collaboration allows the crocodile brand to showcase the sport of its founder, René Lacoste, and reconnects with its original audience. Indeed, tennis retains a special place within the brand as the sport that created the first Lacoste polo shirt.

ROLAND-GARROS COLLECTION

SPRING / SUMMER 2018

(Continued)

Image 5.6 *Lacoste & Roland Garros*

CONSUMER TESTIMONY

Emilie, 34-years-old, married, one child, operation manager, French, Le Slip Français (a French underwear brand) & Racing 92 (a French rugby club) (interviewed in December 2018)

I've been married to my husband for seven years now. I love him so much and think he has almost all the qualities I've always dreamt of. Almost, because in spite of his style, he never made any effort to wear sexy or at least decent lingerie. He can spend hundreds of euros on a coat, but still gets his underwear at low-cost distributors. I felt like he needed to be pushed a little bit so I started looking for something that could be sexy and yet effortless. He's very sporty so I started looking for the product that could create an interest for him. As I was looking through the Internet, I saw an ad for Le Slip Français, they had made a collaboration with Roland-Garros. I had an illumination: that was the underwear I was looking for! The brandname "Roland Garros" is very discreet on the underwear, so it doesn't ruin the general aspect of it. My husband was very happy because this product represented everything he cared about: sporty, convenient, comfortable.... The magic occurred and he started wearing this brand. He couldn't be happier than when Le Slip Français announced a collaboration with Racing 92 lately.... And I couldn't be more happy than seeing my husband wearing fine underwear!

TRANSCEND POTENTIAL MISCONCEPTIONS

- A brand collaboration with sports is one of the most effective brand collaborations for employee motivation and buy-in. It brings employees strong values around team spirit and perseverance.
- Brand collaborations with sports may involve an image risk linked to the behaviour of the athlete or the team (for example, doping problems).
- Brand collaborations with sports may be risky in terms of expected media impact. This risk is particularly related to the uncertainty of sports results.

PEUGEOT

INTERVIEW WITH ISABEL SALAS MENDEZ
Direction marketing and communication

"Why the brand needs to play a logical role in the partnership"

Keywords: long term

Actors: Peugeot, tennis

Peugeot is a French automotive manufacturer founded in 1810 by the family Peugeot itself. Peugeot has received many international awards for its vehicles, including five "European Car of the Year" awards. Peugeot is renowned as a very reliable brand. In 2016, the brand sold around 2 million vehicles. Today it is part of the Groupe PSA which consists includes Citroen, DS, Opel, and Vauxhall.

Tennis is played by millions of players and is a popular worldwide spectator sport. The ATP World Tour is the global elite men's professional tennis circuit organized by the Association of Tennis Professionals (ATP). Its calendar includes Grand Slam tournaments – including Roland Garros Tournament with over 60 million European viewers – the ATP World Tour Master 1000, the ATP World Tour 500 & 250 series, and the ATP finals.

1) How does your collaboration work?

Peugeot has been associated at an international level with three sports: tennis, golf, and rugby. In 2013, we told ourselves that Peugeot should be coherent worldwide to pass on the same values and image. To be able to fully concentrate on one asset, we had to choose which sport best represented the company and its target audience. In order to standardize our partnerships locally and globally, we decided to focus on tennis and stop all other contracts (in rugby, golf, football, basketball etc.). After football, which we thought was over-saturated, and the Olympics, too expansive and not annual, tennis was the third most followed sport.

We became platinum partners of the ATP World Tour and the partner of 35 tournaments worldwide. It's a good way to have an active window of involvement from January until November every year. We have visibility on the court, the referee's chair, the tarpaulins, and on our cars "Peugeot, official partner of …" Depending on the size of the tournament, our brand is present in TV spots broadcast inside the tennis courts. We have tickets for our clients. We also have a corporate hospitality space to receive our clients and our guests. We have a space outside to exhibit our vehicles. All tournaments are equipped with our cars: from 16 to 230 cars depending on the size of the tournament.

For tennis players, we will usually put the Peugeot logo on their sleeve or anywhere for it to be visible when playing the match. Obviously, they will drive a Peugeot vehicle. They have a fixed contract where they will dedicate a number of days to Peugeot to create advertisements for the brand, meet with our clients, be present at products demonstrations etc.

2) What were Peugeot's expectations when collaborating with the tennis world?

Our key markets with the G5 car are Europe, China who became a priority recently with Asia in general, and South America. The United States and Canada are not part of our targeted market yet. As for our age target, it is very large: 18-years-old to the day they cannot drive anymore!

Our clients are mixed, it depends on the product. Hence tennis was a good choice as it is a sport that is followed 51% by men and 49% by women – it is a very mixed sport. We worked with Roland Garros, a French tennis tournament, as well as the ATP World Tour and its 35 tournaments worldwide and a dozen ambassador players. For example, Novak Djokovic, the tennis player, was signed when China was our biggest market as he is a huge celebrity there. He did specific advertising campaigns for the Chinese market. Djokovic was perfect as Chinese celebrities are very expensive and also not very active in tennis. We also partnered with the Miami Open, even though we are not present in the US, as 90% of the viewers are not Americans but are mostly South Americans.

3) What did this partnership bring to the tennis players you collaborated with?

It is a paid partnership. The players, as well as the tournaments in general, are provided with a private chauffeur in a Peugeot for any transportation needed during the tournaments. Djokovic was very happy to collaborate – he lives in Monte Carlo and knows and uses the brand. The values we share corresponded with him and how he portrays himself: a demanding personality, the appearance he gives, and the emotions he shares, especially when playing tennis.

4) What were the fruits of the collaboration and what did it bring to Peugeot in the end?

The tennis competitions were shown worldwide and gave us bigger visibility than our advertisements. We created the programme "Drive to Roland Garros." It consists of unique interviews with the players during their car rides. We distribute it to all channels that broadcast Roland Garros. It is something new and original that is different from the typical press conference and people love it. It attracted 380 million viewers on TV and 10 million views online in two weeks! And we get product placement from our logo on the car's doors where the interview takes place.

We also made a limited-edition Roland Garros 108 car. This 108 is customized with the Roland Garros logo. It is an exclusive product, with only a few produced, which brings a special value to the product. It was a huge success with tennis fans.

We always try to renew our partnerships and do something new with tennis – this seems to be working. We got two awards for strategy for our tennis advertisements.

5) Who worked on this collaboration?

Our marketing and communication team at Peugeot, as well as the ambassador players and their agents, and the communication team of the tournaments.

6) Overall, what were the best parts of the partnership?

Peugeot's association with the tennis world was very well received by all tennis fans. They liked the interviews we've made and the limited editions we've created. Another positive part was the sympathy and the good feeling we had with everyone we worked with – including internally, which is also very important!

7) And the more difficult parts of the partnership?

I would say that the most difficult part is renewing and finding new ideas for advertisements. We have been partnering with Roland Garros for 34 years and we have found some unique ideas like "Drive to Roland Garros." A lot of brainstorming is needed to still innovate with programs like this after 34 years. However, we don't create new products for Roland Garros every year. We restyle older products and will launch some new products around every three years.

8) What do you believe were the keys of success of this partnership?

Natural, innovative programmes and a long-term partnership. I believe that for a partnership to be successful and for people to make the connection between the brand, the celebrity and the product, the partnership must be long-lasting. If we do a one-year partnership, people forget about it, it is useless. Whereas for a ten-year partnership, we associate the values of the brand with the product.

Overall, partnerships are good but what is important is how they are activated! When I say activated, I don't just mean advertisement but also innovation. We try to put players in unusual situations and also mix celebrities from different sectors in our advertising. For example, we mix tennis players with singers, which doubles the fan base. Lastly, it is very important that the brand plays a logical role in the partnership in question. For example, we transport the players and Lacoste dresses the referees.

9) What parts of the partnership could have been improved?

We also had to partner with other personalities as even though tennis as a big audience, it only consists of tennis viewers! We are also reviewing our partnerships strategies to make them more eco-friendly in order to coordinate with our new vehicle range.

Image 5.7 *Peugeot & Roland Garros*

Image 5.8 *Peugeot & Roland Garros*

Image 5.9 *Peugeot & Mika*

Image 5.10 *Peugeot & Mika*

INTERVIEW WITH CARLOS FLEMING
Partner at Endeavor, Sports Talent Group Head (WME)

"Agent of high-profile athletes manages the careers of 20-year-old millionaires; athletes are businesses of their own!"

Keywords: planning long-term, strong ability to sell

Actors: Carlos Fleming for WME, sports athletes

Originally founded in 1960, IMG was acquired by WME in 2014, and together, they formed Endeavor. Now a global leader in sports, events, media, and fashion, operating in more than 30 countries, the company represents and manages some of the world's greatest sports figures and fashion icons, stages hundreds of live events and brand entertainment experiences annually, and is one of the largest independent producers and distributors of sports media. IMG also specializes in sports training, league development, marketing/media, and licensing for brands, sports organizations, and collegiate institutions.

Carlos Fleming is based in New York. Since 1996, Carlos has managed the careers of several high-profile athletes, including Venus Williams (tennis), Victor Oladipo (NBA), Jo Wilfried Tsonga (tennis), Cam Newton (football), Colin Kaepernick (football), Michelle Wie (golf), and many more.

1) What was one of your most successful partnership deals? An endorsement deal that you are particularly fond of and why? What were the challenges?

We did a deal with Cam Newton, who is an American professional football player and an ambassador for the sportswear brand Under Armour. It was interesting because it came along in 2011, when football players were not heavily featured in brand advertising. Under Armour had the vision to use

Cam to gain relevance in the lifestyle market and build their reputation as a football performance brand. The deal we negotiated included signature apparel, signature footwear, philanthropic support, and opportunities for Cam to grow his non-NFL interests.

Also, launching Venus Williams' clothing line in 2012, EleVen, was an interesting project because we created something that Venus was passionate about, with an infrastructure that allowed us to establish the brand with a committed national distribution. Developing the Williams' Sisters Tours in the US and Africa was also very rewarding – these were projects that allowed for creativity, developing personal passion projects, having learning experiences, supporting people in need, and running profitable projects.

As for challenges, I would say managing the careers of 20-year-old celebrity millionaires who control the success of significant organizations has its inherent challenges. The athletes are on a steep learning curve in an intense media spotlight, and they will make mistakes. Our job is to advise and help them anticipate, but also let their personal character and spirit shine through. This is oftentimes a lot easier said than done.

2) You have been in the sports agent business for a while now – how would you say your role as an agent has evolved?

The sports industry has evolved throughout my career. A consistent theme is that advertisers are looking for opportunities to capitalize on the excitement around sports, as well as opportunities to differentiate their brand. In this era of digital advertising, the impact of traditional advertising is becoming increasingly diluted, and some advertisers are taking an even more serious look at marketing their brands through sports affiliations. The passion points that attract fans are becoming vehicles to target core consumers. Sports marketing has changed from "nice to have" for many companies to an important part of their overall brand strategy.

Athletes are becoming increasingly strategic, so agents have had to become much more strategic, too – that's one big change. The superstar athlete has become more focused on developing their post-career business interests, and strategic business partnerships are playing a more prominent role than ever before. There was a time when athletes were proactively looking for marketing opportunities to build their personal brands through partner brand marketing campaigns. This current generation of athletes is becoming much more selective about which brands they will put their names behind. "Authenticity" is a common theme that both athletes and brands use. Furthermore, they are passing on more and more fee-based endorsement deals in exchange for opportunities with early stage companies, venture capital investments, and other equity driven opportunities.

Another big change is the importance of content creation – social media and digital content. Athletes are realizing that they have the ability to become content creators, not unlike traditional television networks. They can share their latest news with millions of fans, which will get picked up and shared by those fans and media outlets with millions more people. They can produce television shows and curate content on platforms like YouTube. From a communications and business perspective, this transition is already having an enormous impact. One must only look at LeBron James' "Uninterrupted" or Derek Jeter's "The Players Tribune." Platforms owned by celebrity athletes that distribute unfiltered content are positioned to become lucrative businesses.

3) Part of your role is also to scout for new talent?

That's correct. You always have to keep looking for ways to grow. There are two ways you can do that – one of them is by growing the business interests of current high-profile athletes/talents already in our portfiolio, and the other is by bringing in new, more high-profile athletes/talents (we also call them "clients"). I would assume the approach is similar in most businesses – to always be thinking about what's next and who's next.

4) What are the differences and similarities between closing deals with well-known athletes and Hollywood celebrities?

Entertainers are entering areas that were historically the focus of athletes and vice versa. When I started, a celebrity actor would most likely not be seen endorsing consumer products in US advertising. Now we see George Clooney selling coffee and Matthew McConaughey selling cars and Samuel L. Jackson selling credit cards. Corporate endorsements like this were once primarily the domain of athletes, but now we are seeing more and more entertainment celebrities enter the space. Conversely, athletes are making headway in areas that were once reserved for celebrities with a focus in entertainment. Athletes are becoming prominent subjects of television programming, executive producing film and television content, financing film projects, producing entertainment events, developing musical artists, and more. The worlds are colliding and the entertainment and sports experts are collaborating more than ever before. This is why we feel that our company is so well positioned in this current generation.

5) Do you think the type of offers you've received over the past five to ten years have changed? Where are brands looking for more content and well-known personalities, trying to differentiate themselves?

We are in a generation where content rules. Social media following is important because of the impressions that athletes can single-handedly generate. As a result, the approach from media companies is often times guided by the ability to create interesting digital content and potential impressions through social media. Offers are much more diverse and range from traditional advertising to offers solely for social posting. This approach, in many cases, means that brands are spending less on any one individual and spreading their spend across more talent.

6) Do you see a big difference between European deals and US deals? If so, why?

In Europe I think we still see a bit more of a traditional structure, although the migration to digital media is a global trend.

And what about Asia? It depends on what country in Asia we're talking about. If we're talking China, their e-commerce market is much more sophisticated than even what we have in the States. Many Asian markets, like Korea, Japan and China, can be incredibly lucrative for domestic talent. Many of our highest paying clients are from Asian countries.

7) How do you see your job evolving in the next ten to twenty years? Is there going to be another shift?

I think the biggest shift is seeing a generation of athletes becoming business people. I think you're going to start to see athletes have teams and build businesses that could range from investment to content production. Salaries are rising and star athletes have access to more capital than ever before. This is allowing athletes to staff up and think more strategically about their brands and business futures. You will see more wealth creation and more athletes that enter nine and ten figure net worth territory.

8) *So in a way, your role throughout time is only expanding. Before you were very niche, now you're opening up and participating in marketing and strategy. You have to be good in sales, good in finding new talents, etc.*

Yes, it is definitely a matter of perspective. You have to be able to see the entire business and anticipate what is next. From a recruiting perspective to a managing perspective, you have to be able to see more global points of view.

9) *Do you think there is a big difference between how you/your company are doing your job and how other companies do theirs? Are there some specificities or do all agencies do it the same way?*

I feel fortunate for the company I work for because we have a diverse group of best in class people in different disciplines. We have the #1 TV agency in Hollywood, the #1 literary team, and a best in class digital team. This makes us more efficient and effective; more strategic and forward thinking.

10) *You have a legal department in your company – I assume you close the deals and then your legal partner will write down the contract, right?*

Yes, we negotiate the business terms and our legal department will come and cover the legal terms. Because of the scope of our agency, we have a library of contracts. We have an array of negotiated sponsorship deals, so we know the best practices on different deal points that are the best available.

11) *Do you foresee a larger scope of personalities, people you're representing?*

Yes, definitely.

12) *You now see more and more personalities partnering with a good cause. Do you also represent good causes, helping them to expand? How do you feel about these partnerships, since the royalties may go to the cause and not*

to the agent? How do you view this increase in charity work and those who wish to help them?

We do a really good job at prioritizing giving back to the community; we have a foundation where UNICEF is one of our primary partners. In addition, we're always on the front lines of community projects, whether it's dealing with US gun control tragedies, in and outside of school, or female empowerment movements. We've done a good job of ensuring cultural diversity within several communities. My personal philosophy has always been if you do good in the community, both as an athlete and in business, then you'll always be good. Foundation work is often part of a person's strategy as well, which you have to stay focused on. I think that's another reason a lot of athletes and celebrities say no a lot to different organizations; they have to maximize their impact, and it's a very narrow lane.

13) What is your dream endorsement to do in the upcoming years? Which brand or personality are you really looking forward to work with?

It would be to help our artists and athletes launch a brand, that would be really interesting, something that could be viable and last over a long period of time.

REFERENCES

Blackett, T. and Russell, N. (1999). What is Co-branding? In *Co-Branding* (pp. 1–21). Palgrave Macmillan, London.

Burlot, F. and Pichot, L. (2004). *L'événement sportif et la cohésion des salariés en entreprise* (No. hal-01754803).

Do, H., Ko, E. and Woodside, A.G. (2015). Tiger Woods, Nike, and I are (not) best friends: How brand's sports sponsorship in social-media impacts brand consumer's congruity and relationship quality. *International Journal of Advertising, 34*(4), 658–677.

Motion, J., Leitch, S. and Brodie, R.J. (2003). Equity in corporate co-branding: The case of Adidas and the All Blacks. *European Journal of Marketing, 37*(7/8), 1080–1094.

Pierre, J. and Tribou, G. (2013). L'événementiel sportif comme outil de communication interne en entreprise. *Gestion 2000, 30*(3), 113–128.

CHAPTER 6

Brand collaborations with Good Causes

Corporate social responsibility considers the impact of a company's activities on different stakeholders (clients, employees, citizen, suppliers, retailers, local communities, etc.). Beyond corporate social responsibility, companies engage their brands more frequently in good causes not directly linked with their commercial activities or products. For instance, the beer brand, Leffe, financed the renovation of the San Benedetto Basilica after the Norcia earthquake (Italy, 2017) – 100,000 limited-edition bottles of the beer were sold in Italy and the profits were donated to the monks of the Basilica. This collaboration allowed Leffe beer to reconnect with its roots. Companies act beyond their products because they want their brands to become well known in social and environment spheres and not just in economic spheres. Nowadays, companies legitimately to use their brands to communicate their social commitments to consumers. This tendency is increasing for a variety of companies (large and small companies) and in different sectors (BtoB and BtoC).

Table 6.1 Brand collaborations with Good causes

Kinds of llaboration	Definition	Examples
o-branded oducts and duct-sharing	Collaboration between a brand and an NGO involving the launching of a new product with or without a sale percentage redistributed to the NGO	- Pampers & UNICEF - Leffe & Basilique San Benedetto - Levi's & Fondation Harvey Milk
o-branded munication	Collaboration between a brand and an NGO involving common communication to make the public aware about the work of the NGO	- Bonobo Jeans & Solidarité Sida - Estee Lauder & Pink ribbon - Coca-Cola & WWF - H&M & WWF

6.1 WHEN BRANDS CREATE PRODUCTS FOR THE BENEFIT OF NGOS

For many years now, brands have collaborated environmentally and ethically with NGOs as a means of expression and of socio-political engagement. Sometimes collaborations with non-profit organizations can generate the creation of new products highlighting the partnership. For instance, Lacoste have signed a partnership with The International Union for the Conservation of Nature (IUCN), one of the most important and diversified environmental networks in the world, with a mission to protect nature in all its forms. Lacoste financially supports the operation "Save Our Species" a project initiated with the mission to saving endangered species. To show their engagement, Lacoste launched an exclusive capsule collection of polo shirts on which the iconic Lacoste crocodile was replaced by ten other animals, each featuring an endangered species such as the rhinoceros, parakeet or tiger. Each polo shirt (€150), created in collaboration with Save Our Species, was available in numbers according to how many of the animals are known to be still alive, in total 1,775. The polo shirts were sold out in 24 hours!

Burberry demonstrated its support to the LGBTQ (Lesbian, Gay, Bisexual, Transgender, Queer) community. Burberry committed to the ideology that "Everyone is equal" and refashioned the British house's signature tartan with a rainbow twist and added it to the label's classic caps, bags, and other outerwear pieces. Burberry unveiled these capsule collection pieces while announcing their donations to three charities – The Albert Kennedy Trust, The Trevor Project and ILGA – which are all dedicated to spreading awareness and acceptance of the LGBTQ community.

Similarly, every year, Levi's creates a Pride collection to celebrate their friends and family in the LGBTQ community. For the American brand,

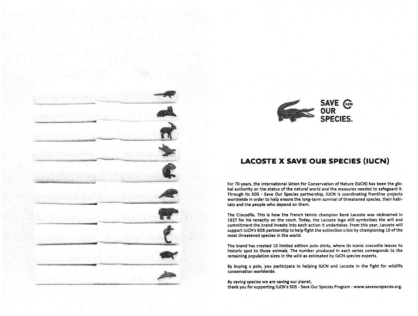

SAVE OUR SPECIES.

LACOSTE X SAVE OUR SPECIES (IUCN)

For 70 years, the International Union for Conservation of Nature (IUCN) has been the global authority on the status of the natural world and the measures needed to safeguard it. Through its SOS – Save Our Species partnership, IUCN is coordinating frontline projects worldwide in order to help ensure the long-term survival of threatened species, their habitats and the people who depend on them.

The Crocodile. This is how the French tennis champion René Lacoste was nicknamed in 1927 for his tenacity on the court. Today, the Lacoste logo still symbolises the will and commitment the brand invests into each action it undertakes. From this year, Lacoste will support IUCN's SOS partnership to help fight the extinction crisis by championing 10 of the most threatened species in the world.

The brand has created 10 limited edition polo shirts, where its iconic crocodile leaves its historic spot to those animals. The number produced in each series corresponds to the remaining population sizes in the wild as estimated by IUCN species experts.

By buying a polo, you participate in helping IUCN and Lacoste in the fight for wildlife conservation worldwide.

By saving species we are saving our planet, thank you for supporting IUCN's SOS - Save Our Species Program - www.saveourspecies.org.

Image 6.1 *Lacoste & Save our spicies*

t's a way to increase visibility, get more people involved in the push for equality and give back to society. Made with self-expression in mind, the 2018 collection celebrates the many ways people can customize their Levi's and centred their designs around the "I AM" tee as a way to encourage people to put their unique style on display. In addition to the collection, Levi's wanted to show how members of the LGBTQ community live their lives. To do that, they presented, on their website, videos asking some pioneers and activists to share their stories.

Balenciaga also demonstrates its support for the NGO World Food Program during catwalks. Logos of the NGO (WFP) are shown by the models during the luxury catwalks. Just as luxury houses support NGOs, it seems that, nowadays, the logos of NGOs can be visible fashion signs on luxury clothes.

Supporting good causes and showing your commitment can be done through product-sharing – the skincare company, Kiehl's, supports the foundation "Arbres Canada" which helps the reforestation of disaster areas across the country. To support this cause, Kiehl's launched a new collection of cosmetic products and for each product sold, Kiehl's is committed to planting a tree in the stricken areas of Canada. Kiehl's also collaborates with actor Matthew McConaughey to support the Autism Speaks organization. The collaboration is centred around a special video of the actor spreading the message that "children with autism need our support and they need it right now." Viewers are invited to share the informative video across all social media platforms to raise awareness and money for funding autism research and resources. For every share the video receives, Kiehl's donates $1 to Autism Speaks until they reach their goal of $200,000 (for more information see the interview of the Kiehl's CEO at the end of this chapter).

In the fashion market, the Japanese clothing brand Uniqlo and French pastry Ladurée have joined forces for a charity project in benefit of child victims of the 2011 earthquake in Japan. Together, the two brands are launching a capsule collection of t-shirts for children and women. Six different models are available, all in Ladurée's signature pastel colours, and part of the profit from sales will be donated to help children affected by the tsunami.

It is not possible to speak about product-sharing without speaking of the collaboration between Pampers and UNICEF. Pampers, one of the most famous brands of diapers for babies, has supported UNICEF since 2006 by devoting a percentage of their diaper sales to the NGO. The last brand collaboration, across a selection of Pampers nappies and wipes, the brand's '1 Pack = 1 Vaccine' campaign, helped UNICEF to eliminate maternal and new-born tetanus. An estimated 500,000 new-born babies have been saved and a vaccine has reached a mother and her baby every second since the Pampers-UNICEF partnership began in 2006. The main advantage of this kind of collaboration is the transfer of an affective dimension from the NGO and the brand (Dickinson and Barker, 2007). Additionally, the high fit between Pampers products and UNICEF's mission towards children makes the collaboration relevant (Lafferty, 2009).

Image 6.2 *Louis Vuitton & UNICEF*

Louis Vuitton has renewed its partnership with UNICEF to fight against diseases, natural disasters, conflicts, and other threats that endanger children around the world. For the occasion, the French luxury brand has designed a pendant ($600) and a bracelet ($500) to support UNICEF's actions to improve and promote the condition of children. For every Silver Lockit bracelet sold, Louis Vuitton has donated $200 to UNICEF. This collaboration is part of a global partnership between Louis Vuitton and UNICEF which has allowed them to collect more than $5 million in two years to support the emergency programmes of UNICEF.

In the jewellery sector, Chopard supports the Naked Heart Foundation created by supermodel Natalia Vodianova. This support has been accompanied by the creation of a special edition of Happy Hearts jewellery around the theme of generosity which is important for the brand. A part of the profits goes to the foundation to help children with disabilities and special needs.

Despite the success of some partnerships between luxury brands and good causes, luxury brands have to be conscious that the match between luxury

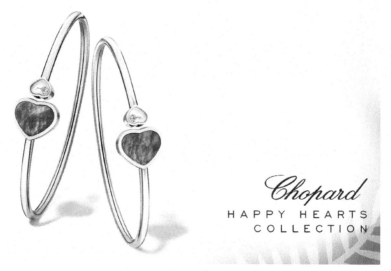

Image 6.3 *Chopard & Happy heart*

and NGOs is not always appreciated. A study reveals that communicating the corporate social responsibility actions of a luxury brand can be perceived negatively (Torelli, 2011). One of the typical values of luxury brands such as *self-enhancement* (i.e. dominance over people and resources) is in conflict with the *self-transcendence* value (i.e. protecting the welfare of all) that is the main value of corporate social responsibility. Hence, collaborations between luxury brands and NGOs can be perceived as not legitimate and generate a negative opinion about luxury brands accused of greenwashing.

Within the product-sharing strategy, the makeup brand Beautiful Rights has developed an interesting form of brand collaboration with good causes – the makeup brand donates 20% of its sales to the women's rights charity chosen by each customer on purchase. The idea is that when consumers make a purchase, they choose where they want their money to go from the list of six organizations proposed by the brand: Planned Parenthood, the ACLU, MomsRising, Emily's list, Lambda Legal, or Legal Momentum.

EXAMPLE: MAX HAVELAAR FAIRTRADE LABELLING (CERTIFICATION)

The strategy of labelling brands can be considered as a brand collaboration (Larceneux et al., 2012). For brands, the principle of this kind of collaboration is to use a label from an independent organization through adopting its specifications. Major labelling organizations (such as Max Havelaar or World Wide Fund), in spite of not being corporate brands per se, promote their own name and compete with other organizations. Max Havelaar certification competes with other organizations and federations operating with their own labels (e.g. ECOCERT Equitable, Fair for Life, FairWild, Forest Garden Products, Naturland Fair and WFTO). Their strategy is based on brand alliances with commercial brands. In this kind of brand collaboration, the commercial brand (host brand) brings its own brand awareness, associated with quality and innovation. Reciprocally, the labelling brand (the guest brand) provides the consumer with a Fairtrade value, a safety and ethical guarantee that goes beyond the level brands can usually offer (Senechal et al., 2013). The brand obtains the Fairtrade certification if it fulfils the Fairtrade certification conditions. Certification, such as Max Havelaar, enhances the image and the evaluation of the brand. More specifically, one of the main benefits of this labelling is a Fairtrade orientation – proving fair working conditions, greater benefits to producers, guaranteeing a safe workplace, as well as a fair price that covers the cost of production and facilitates social development and protection of the environment (Cailleba and Casteran, 2010; Larceneux et al., 2012).

A study (Senechal et al., 2013) shows that, in the context of Fairtrade labelling, inconsistency may be more useful than consistency for the memorization and global evaluation of the co-branded product. Specifically, moderate levels of similarity between both brands seem to improve consumers' attitudes towards the co-branded product and are likely to enhance the corporate brands perception as delivering corporate social responsibility (CSR). This finding demonstrates that managers should not be afraid of pursuing collaborations with Fairtrade labels, as dissimilarity and surprise positively impact consumers' evaluations.

6.2 WHEN BRANDS EXPRESS THEIR SUPPORT FOR GOOD CAUSES

When brands collaborate with good causes, they can decide to make their partnership visible without launching new products. For instance, to show that FC Barcelona has given €2 million a year to UNICEF and has reached more than one million children in seven countries over ten years, they made a video taking a look back at their ten-year-old partnership. This kind of advertisement demonstrates the role of sport as a source of values, the involvement of the players, and FC Barcelona's positioning as the Club of the Children. The two organizations are conscious of using sport as a social and educational tool in order to work in the awareness, detection, and prevention of HIV/AIDS. From the point of view of FC Barcelona, this partnership with UNICEF focused on the social commitment to children which has meaning for the players. This collaboration demonstrates that FC Barcelona practices what it preaches.

The communication about the partnership between a brand and an NGO can be more discreet and less connected with the commercial activities of the brand. For example, the fashion group PVH Corp, owners of Calvin Klein and Tommy Hilfiger amongst others, has teamed up with WWF, an NGO dedicated to protecting the environment and working for sustainable

Image 6.4 *H&M & WWF*

development. Because water is used at every stage of their product lifecycle, the company PVH recognizes its responsibility in taking a lead role in addressing the pressing global issue of water supply and their goal is to conserve water in Africa and India. Their two main brands (Calvin Klein and Tommy Hilfiger) play a key role in the conservation of freshwater resources in Lake Awasa in Ethiopia and in the River Cauvery in India.

In the same vein, WWF and H&M group have joined forces to focus on water issues. The partnership has begun to transform H&M's internal water management system as well as engaging suppliers, policy makers, NGOs, communities, and other companies to collectively advocate for more sustainable water use in specific areas in Asia.

This collaboration suggests that in a cause–brand alliance, the fit between the brand and the NGO is not the central key to its success (Austin & Seitanidi, 2012) – the most important thing is the credibility of the brand in supporting the cause. A study focusing on the cause–brand alliance (Laferty, 2007) has shown that to explain consumer's purchase intention of the brand, the most important thing is not the fit between the cause and the brand but the brand level of credibility. The findings suggest we need to re-think fit as a necessary selection criterion for a cause–brand alliance. Concerning the impact of the collaboration between brands and NGOs, it appears that the collaboration improves the perception of unpopular NGOs but did not change the opinion on ones that are already well-known. This result suggests that managers of lesser-known NGOs, rather than popular NGOs, may have the greater interest in forming brand collaborations (Lafferty, Goldsmith and Hult, 2004).

BRAND ACTIVISM AS A KIND OF BRAND COLLABORATION

In response to social and environmental issues, companies have begun to take a more active role in involving themselves into political and humanitarian causes. The role of corporations is evolving, and, for example, Unilever's CEO Paul Polman states, "if you want to exist as a company in the future, you have to go beyond. You actually have to make a positive contribution."[1] In fact, studies show that investing in socially conscious positioning has the potential to increase customer loyalty, revenue, and brand recall. According to an Edelman Earned Brand study (2018), 64% of consumers around the world will buy or boycott a brand solely because of its position on a social or political issue.[2] Kantar Consulting's new Purpose 2020 report shows 80% of American customers are more loyal to purpose-driven brands. With this knowledge, more and more brands are using activism in their messaging. In 2018 alone, many brands put this to use. Nike partnered with football player Colin Kaepernick to highlight the American Black Lives Matter movement. The beer company Stella Artois, NGO Water.org, and actor Matt Damon joined together to promote Save Water during a 2018 Super Bowl advertisement. In another collaboration, Smirnoff vodka and music application Spotify tackled gender inequality in music, analysing customer downloads and suggesting an equal percentage of men and women performers. The list of collaborations using brand activism continues to grow, and the future is sure to see more partnerships fighting for good causes.

1 Interview of Paul Polman the chief executive officer of Unilever by Rik Kirkland, McKinsey Publishing's senior managing editor interview: www.mckinsey.com/business-functions/sustainability/our-insights/business-society-and-the-future-of-capitalism
2 Edelman Earned Brand study (2018), Brands take a stand: www.edelman.com/sites/g/files/aatuss191/files/2018-10/2018_Edelman_Earned_Brand_Global_Report.pdf

ESTÉE LAUDER COMPANIES
CAMPAGNE DE LUTTE
CONTRE LE CANCER DU SEIN

Cancer du Sein
Tous concernés !

#TimeToEndBreastCancer
#parlonsen
www.cancerdusein.org
pinkribbonaward.fr
ELCompanies.com/BreastCancerCampaign

Image 6.5 *Estée Lauder & Breast Cancer Research Foundation*

To illustrate how brands are committed to social causes beyond their products, we can mention the pink ribbon of Estée Lauder. In 1992, Evelyn Lauder, Vice President of Estée Lauder Companies, created the Pink Ribbon, recognized today as the international symbol of the awareness campaign on the importance of the early detection of breast cancer. At the same time, Evelyn Lauder decided to help the world's leading medical and scientific researchers and created the Breast Cancer Research Foundation (BCRF) to support research. This commitment also continues with the sale of limited-edition products sold for the benefit of the cause and the creation of the Estée Lauder Awards. More than € 2,240,000 has already been donated to breast cancer research since the first edition of the Pink Ribbon Awards in 2004.

Partnering charitable causes with brands has become a common practice for many marketing programs, referred to strategically as cause-related marketing. Hence, for brand managers these collaborations with Good causes are beneficial in terms of brand image and NGOs always need a more financial support. However, it is important to ensure a good consistency between the brand and the good cause to avoid negative consequences (Sabri, 2018). For instance, even if a brand is committed to supporting NGOs that fight against breast cancer, some of their products can contain ingredients that are potentially carcinogenic. This kind of inconsistency is rejected today by consumers who have the power to denounce the brand's dishonesty.

CONSUMER TESTIMONY

Leslie, 34-years-old, married, one child, human resources manager, French, Lush (a cosmetic brand) and Animal Rights

It took me a while to start using skincare products. I told myself at first that I didn't need them, I wanted to be special somehow. When I turned 30, I understood that it was not possible to leave my face without any care and it would prejudice me one day or another. When I looked for a shop, I didn't know where to start. I was already used to organic food and responsible consuming. I didn't see myself buying Nivea or L'Occitane, in spite of their good reputation. When I learnt about Lush, I knew that was something for me. I think I didn't want to take care of myself without thinking about someone else, I would have felt guilty. I feel so privileged to have everything I have today. Lush fights animal testing and sells special pots called "charity pots," which is basically a standard moisturizing cream, from which all the benefits go to goodwill and charity. I believe this is the best way to take care of myself. As I often go to the shop, I have the opportunity to see every time the NGO they are working for at the moment, because it changes a lot. I know my purchase helps someone somewhere and that's a real difference for me. On top of that, as the products are efficient, I wouldn't change for any other brand.

TRANSCEND POTENTIAL MISCONCEPTIONS

Luxury brands can collaborate with NGOs when their values and activities fit with the values of the NGO.
Collaborations between brands and NGOs enrich both partners.
However, these collaborations do not equally profit all NGOs or causes. Less popular NGOs draw greater benefits from a collaboration with a brand than already established ones.

SINCE 1851

INTERVIEW WITH CHERYL VITALI AND ANNA BORGOGNI

General manager worldwide, Kiehl's

Global communication, Kiehl's

"Giving back to our community is fundamental in a successful good cause related partnership"

Keywords: giving back

Actors: Kiehl's, Matthew McConaughey, Autism Speaks

Kiehl's is a skin care company, selling premium hair, skin and body products, and became part of L'Oreal group in the year 2000. Founded in 1851 in New York's East Village, Kiehl's currently operates in over 500 retail stores and 2,200 points of sales worldwide. For more than 160 years, Kiehl's has a legacy of bringing exposure to under-represented causes and is committed to supporting its local communities.

Matthew McConaughey, born in 1969, is an American actor, producer, model, writer, and director. He's earned several awards and was named Best Actor for his role as a cowboy diagnosed with AIDS in *Dallas Buyers Club*. McConaughey supports many good causes and has his own foundation for helping children. He has also partnered with many different brands – from Dolce & Gabbana perfume, to Lincoln cars, to Campari – to help raise funds and awareness for these causes.

Autism Speaks is an NGO dedicated to researching and providing tools for the needs of people and children with autism. Visit autismspeaks.org to learn more.

1) How did Kiehl's announce the collaboration?

In September 2017, Kiehl's announced the collaboration with Matthew McConaughey to benefit Autism Speaks, a global leader in autism advocacy. Kiehl's created a launch event in NYC show casing their co-created video. The video was posted on their mutual social media and helped raise awareness and spread the message "Children with autism need your attention right now." For each video shared on social media, Kiehl's donated $1. In total the brand committed to a maximum of $200K to be donated to the good cause. The partnership also included a limited edition of one of Kiehl's bestselling facial cream co-created by the actor, the brand, and the autism cause.

2) What were Kiehl's expectations for the partnership?

Having a guest star such as Matthew McConaughey is a way to give more visibility to our message and the cause we support. On the customer side, it also gives an extra dimension to the celebrity, and the limited edition he/she supports. However, who benefits the most is probably the cause, the philanthropic association, because that is generally what ties us together. With this partnership, we will continue our legacy, using our global Kiehl's network to help raise awareness for children and families affected by autism.

For over 160 years, Kiehl's has been committed to supporting the communities in which we serve our customers. We have a legacy of bringing exposure to underrepresented causes. Our founder, Aaron Morse, said "part of Kiehl's DNA and values is to play a responsible role alongside their customers through civic and environmental initiatives, sponsorships, and localized events." We at Kiehl's do global philanthropic initiatives every two to three years and as a brand, but we do not advertise or hire celebrities. On a local level, every country in the world that has opened a Kiehl's store (64 countries now), is required to have at least one philanthropic initiative per year in line with our brand platform called "Kiehl's gives" and the three causes we support: Children, Environment, or AIDS research.

3) What did this partnership bring to Matthew McConnaughey?

The collaboration amplified Matthew McConaughey's image as a philanthropist.

He has his own foundation: The *JK Livin Foundation*. ("Just Keep Livin" Foundation), a non-profit foundation committed to the health and wellbeing of youth, supporting many programs in the community, such as acting school classes for children. Additionally, his foundation also provides support for children with autism. Being an experienced philanthropist himself, Matthew's interest in collaborating with us was apparent, as he knows how important helping children is to us.

4) What were the fruits of the collaboration?

The partnership includes the release of a Kiehl's and Matthew McConaughey Limited Edition Ultra Facial Cream. He designed the label of the limited edition himself, with vibrant features, uplifting colours and geometric shapes, including interlocking puzzle pieces - a reference to the iconic Autism Speaks blue puzzle-piece logo. Matthew McConaughey brought to the table his worldwide recognition. He offered his photography for retail usage and appearances in the video for free and deployed it on his own social channels. Matthew McConaughey also created a video to raise awareness and spread the message "children with autism need your attention right now." Kiehl's invited patrons to share this special video, and donated $1 per share, up to $200,000, to Autism Speaks. It was an authentic way to widely speak about the association of autism.

5) What do you believe were the keys to the success of this partnership?

It was by far the most successful campaign, in terms of driving awareness, sharing content, that we ever done globally. For autism, it is sometimes difficult for people to give a hand because it is not an easy topic. We've got a lot of additional social content from influencers around the world whether we are associating with autism or because Matthew associates. We don't advertise because people will think that the products are the cause.

6) What parts of the partnership could have been improved?

Your last partnership is always your best one. But every time we collaborate, we get more impressions from the communication and we learn a lot. In regards to our future communications, we can always do better. Making the world a better, healthier place, is very important to Kiehl's and we will continue to look for ways that we think are important and possible for us to achieve our goal. And, yes, I definitely think that there is a next step in the future chapters of Kiehl's collaborations to make better and to give back even more to our communities!

Image 6.6 *Kiehl's gives*

Image 6.7 *Kiehl's & Jeremyville*

INTERVIEW WITH PALOMA ESCUDERO AND MARISSA BUCKANOFF

Director of global communications, Unicef

Chief of celebrity relations, Unicef

"UNICEF's shirt sponsorship deal with BARCA, worth €2 million per season, funded entirely by the football club's members"

Keywords: goodwill ambassadors, charitable partnership with brands

Actors: UNICEF, FC Barcelona (BARCA)

UNICEF stands for the United Nations International Children's Emergency Fund, and it works in 190 countries and territories to protect the rights of every child. For over 70 years, UNICEF has been the defender of children around the world, regardless of gender, religion, race, or economic background.

UNICEF strongly believes in the power of partnerships and collaborative efforts and works closely with multi-national corporations, national companies. and small-to medium-sized businesses to identify, design and implement alliances that leverage the strengths of the corporate sector on behalf of the world's children. In return, UNICEF supports companies that aim to strengthen their commitment towards the mission of the organization; to improve the lives of children and their families through safe shelter, nutrition, disaster and conflict protection, and equality.

UNICEF also calls upon celebrities with a wide range of talents and achievements, who share a commitment of improving the lives of children worldwide. The organization has various types of representation, divided into Goodwill, Regional, and National Ambassadors. Goodwill Ambassadors have a strong international appeal who are influential beyond their national borders. Current members in this role include Katy Perry, Serena Williams, and Liam Neeson. UNICEF has a total of 30 Goodwill ambassadors world-wide. This differs from Regional Ambassadors, who are celebrities with strong regional appeal and work primarily within the region of their recruitment, such as Argentinian artist and illustrator Miguel Repiso, Indian cricket legend Sachin Tendulkar, or former Miss South Pacific, Merewalesi Nailatikau. As for National Ambassadors, these are celebrities with strong local appeal and constituencies, affiliated with National Committees or UNICEF Country Offices, working primarily within the nation of their recruitment. UNICEF National Ambassadors currently represent over 90 countries.

FC Barcelona (BARCA) is a professional football club based in Barcelona, Catalonia, Spain. *Forbes* ranked it the fourth most valuable sports team in the world with a team value of $3.64 billion. It has won 20 European and World titles. Created in 1994, the FC Barcelona Foundation is the organization through which FC Barcelona gives back to the global community. All its projects use sport as a focal point, with the idea of promoting education and civic values amongst children and young adults in Spain and the rest of the world. Currently, the FC Barcelona Foundation programs has more than 300,000 beneficiaries.

1) How was the collaboration between UNICEF and BARCA announced?

FC Barcelona and UNICEF signed their first agreement in September 2006. Ten years later, in 2016, FC Barcelona and UNICEF agreed to extend their alliance for 4 more years, during which FC Barcelona increased its annual donation to €2 million.

The agreement supports the fight against AIDS and implements new projects to foster children's education through sport in the neediest areas of the world while continuing to use sport as a social tool. The collaboration also included incorporating the logo of UNICEF on the FC Barcelona team shirts without cost for UNICEF. The club earns the distinction of being the first sports team ever to use its shirts to advocate for a cause, rather than advertise a commercial sponsor. This was the first placement of its kind in the club's 118-year history and an unprecedented gesture in the world of football.

2) What were UNICEF's expectations for this collaboration with BARCA? And, in general, for all UNICEF's partnerships with goodwill ambassadors and corporate partners?

There were three main objectives for the partnership with BARCA: to reach a new and younger audience; to expand and reinforce UNICEF's message and campaign through sports and social media; and to increase the funding of UNICEF's programmes for children.

In general, UNICEF has a long history of partnering with high profile personalities in order to raise awareness of its mission and the challenges children face around the world. Most of UNICEF's Goodwill Ambassadors represent specialized fields in the arts, sports and contemporary culture. Naturally, there's a difference between Goodwill Ambassadors versus corporate partnerships, such as BARCA. UNICEF Goodwill Ambassadors are volunteers that help focus the world's eyes on the needs of children and support UNICEF's mission to ensure every child's right to health, education, equality and protection. The process of a partnership with Goodwill Ambassadors is also different, taking a lot of time (more than one year) to meet with them and work with them to become the face of UNICEF. The appointment of a Goodwill Ambassador has to be approved/signed by the UNICEF Executive Director.

For instance, UNICEF's partnership with American singer Katy Perry began before she was appointed a Goodwill Ambassador. Prior to her appointment, she travelled to the field to witness UNICEF programs firsthand, as well as attending UNICEF events and providing support to UNICEF campaigns. She seemed to be a great fit because she was young, and could empower women and girls. In addition, she was able to gain a huge amount of attention through her social media (200 million followers). Perry has been a very popular UNICEF ambassador since 2013! In 2011, tennis star Serena Williams was added to the list of UNICEF's Goodwill Ambassadors, focusing on education. Now one of 30 UNICEF Goodwill Ambassadors, Williams brings undeniable star power to UNICEF's image and media visibility. Besides an amazing professional sports career,

Williams has cultivated a strong online social media following with 25 million followers, and is beloved by many. Perhaps these accomplishments explain her positive impact as a UNICEF advocate. Her CNN op-ed regarding the partnership generated over 62 articles, including 42 top-tier media sources, such as *The Telegraph*, *The Guardian*, BBC Sport, *USA Today*, ABC News, HuffPost, *Time Magazine*, Fox News, CNN, Sky Sports, Huffington Post, *El Tiempo*, *El Pais*, People, Entertainment Tonight, and much, much more. This exemplifies the power of partnerships with sports celebrities, as it relates to their ability to attract major attention and visibility to good causes.

Overall, when UNICEF decides to work with a corporate partner, we prefer to have a long-term partnership objective. The idea that we have in mind is that the partner supports UNICEF until the goal has been reached. With the learning skill of the partnership, the partner can decide whether they want to go on and move to another objective to reach next. Therefore, we at UNICEF, always target the founder or CEO of companies we want to collaborate with. People who work long term for a company can be really engaged in projects and can give a bit more insurance that the partnership project will be long term too. Another advantage of a long-term partnership is that the investment and involvement of UNICEF is so big, it would be a pity if it was only for a "one-shot." As a result, UNICEF has many long-standing collaborations, which spans out over a number of years. For example, we've worked in close contact with LEGO since 2015, Unilever and UNIQLO since 2012, Gucci and the bank ING since 2005, and Montblanc and H&M since 2004. All in all, partnerships on a global level require a really proactive attitude. UNICEF's global team needs to be really selective and conduct a lot of research in order to determine who they can work with (the process lasts around 18 months).On the other hand, you'd be surprised by the number of companies approaching UNICEF, especially regarding family-owned companies rooted in specific countries, wanting to engage on a national level, instead of a global partnership. All in all, you always need a dialogue to see what you can do for each other, ensuring a mutually beneficial relationship.

3) What did the BARCA partnership bring to UNICEF? In general, what do partnerships bring to UNICEF?

The partnership with BARCA was a huge success in terms of world-wide publicity, especially in Asia, Latin America, and Africa, and enabled UNICEF to reach a new audience they wouldn't have access to without this partnership. From 2006 to 2010, UNICEF and FC BARCA have worked in Swaziland, Malawi, and Angola in the awareness, detection, and prevention of HIV/AIDS. From 2011, the work has been focused on South Africa, Ghana, Brazil, and China, using football as an educational tool. FC Barcelona has contributed a total of €15 million over the last decade to projects, benefiting more than one million children!

Since the soccer players of FC Barcelona serve as role models to the younger generation, it was a good way to spread the message of UNICEF amongst a younger audience and a male-dominated population. One of the main goals of using celebrities was to reach an audience the organization would not normally reach and get them interested in an issue. Last but not least, since Nike has become the official sponsor of BARCA, this has opened doors for UNICEF to discuss future projects with Nike, such as expanding the network and contacts of the organization.

Of course, UNICEF has participated in dozens of other high-end collaborations, all contributing their own value. While the cooperation with BARCA was a huge success because of the media attention, visibility, and awareness of the club, is it important to note other innovative ways UNICEF has created to value for its brand. In the case of Amadeus, a new digital platform allowed the travel industry to encourage small, individual donations from travellers around the world. During checkout, customers were offered the option to contribute, with the suggested donation prices displayed next to their potential impact. For example, €3 means 6 vaccinations, €10 means 8 children can receive treatment against severe malnourishment, and €20 ensures 6 families have mosquito nets, which help prevent malaria.

Another, different way UNICEF wins through partnerships can be found in the case of Louis Vuitton and World Children Day. Since 2016, the luxury brand collaborates with UNICEF by making a specially designed product, the Silver Lockit bracelets. Selling for €300, €100 of every purchase is directly donated to UNICEF to protect children from danger. The partnership was paired with the hashtag #MAKEAPROMISE, in which supporters could promise to help children by buying products, and posting on social media, encouraging friends (a high-end demographic of potential UNICEF donators) to do the same.

4) In return, what did this collaboration bring to BARCA? And, in general, what do partnerships bring to UNICEF's partners?

FC Barcelona won the Spirit of Sport Award in recognition of this partnership to benefit children across the developing world affected by HIV/AIDS. The Spirit of Sport Award acknowledges those in sports who take action to create a better world. FC Barcelona's innovative decision to raise awareness about the values of UNICEF was honoured as a perfect example of how sports can help the most vulnerable children.

While FC Barcelona gained awards and recognition for do-gooding, other UNICEF partners had different rewards. IKEA, for example, profited in the form of advice and positive public relations. During their 1990s publicity scandal regarding child labour issues, UNICEF provided advice and assistance. This cause-related marketing help allowed IKEA to engage in a charitable and very public conversation, adding to their company's goodwill, legitimacy, credibility, corporate social responsibility, and good press.

Pampers is another illustration of UNICEF's value towards brands. Through its "1 Pack = 1 Vaccine" marketing campaign, Pampers has successfully donated over 300 million tetanus vaccines, protecting more than 100 million women and their children globally. While this clearly helped UNICEF's cause, it was a relationship forged from mutual gratification. This increased their visibility worldwide, and helped solidify their household name status and brand recognition. In terms of a marketing strategy, the goal of the campaign had perfect synergy with the brand, and allowed for real authenticity.

5) Who worked on the BARCA collaboration?

The sponsorship idea itself was introduced to our Spanish team by a very senior person who used to work for UNICEF and after retirement became member of the chair of the national community in Catalonia. He was very close with the BARCA members, and he had a big role in starting this collaboration together with UNICEF's Spanish team. As this sponsorship deal is a global project, we work closely with our teams around the world but in particular it is the Spanish UNICEF team together with our Geneva headquarters and NY offices who handle on a day-to-day basis the project. Then the program has such an impact that all UNICEF countries worldwide work with it and benefit from it!

6) Overall, what were the best parts of the BARCA partnership?

The best part of the partnership with BARCA was the fact that its 200,000 members paid and contributed to the partnership with UNICEF. They felt and showed over the years a very strong commitment to this particular and innovative partnership of their club with the UNICEF's cause. Also, the board and top members of the club showed a strong commitment over the years we have been working together. The football players come and go in a club – they definitely helped us raise the awareness thanks to Barca's and UNICEF branded shirts they wear but the fans, members and the management of the club are long lasting and guaranteed us this success The power of this collaboration resides also on the fact that it has evolved from prevention of HIV in Africa then shifted to education, and now we're focusing together on another new objective! As you can see, ideal partners must have the flexibility to evolve!

7) What were the more difficult parts of the BARCA partnership?

Combating rumours! To the contrary of what almost half of the population thought, UNICEF did not pay FC Barcelona for their sponsorship; it was BARCA members who funded the deal! It was very important for UNICEF to have a very good communication team, due to this public confusion We needed to get the message across of how BARCA's members were generous! The partnership was so innovative and never seen before in the sports industry that we needed to educate the public and make them understand how the deal was made!

8) How do you foresee the future of UNICEF's partnerships?

There's a growing interest emerging from a lot of tech-companies wanting to engage on a global level in terms of the "radiance" of UNICEF projects. In the next ten years, you will see a new generation of CEOs that care a lot and are really dedicated.

Good causes, like children's welfare, will become part of their brand's own DNA, as well as other socially responsible commitments and dedications. UNICEF's long-lasting relationship with Procter & Gamble is a good example. Procter & Gamble previously made a campaign on women's empowerment. Because they have a much higher budget to campaign with, the production and execution was very professional and got the message across perfectly. So future collaborations will not be about putting two logos next to each other, but about sharing the same values, and incorporating good causes' values into the brand and the company!

INTERVIEW WITH DAVID BLOCH
Head of Corporate Marketing Partnership at
WWF International

"How do you raise consumer awareness of responsible forest products?"

Keywords: transformational partnerships

Actors: WWF, Kimberly Clark, Forest Stewardship Council

WWF is an international non-governmental organization founded in 1961. WWF is one of the world's largest and most respected independent conservation organizations, with over 5 million supporters and a global network active in over 100 countries. WWF's mission is to stop the degradation of the earth's natural environment and to build a future in which humans live in harmony with nature, by conserving the world's biological diversity, ensuring the use of renewable natural resources is sustainable, and promoting the reduction of pollution and wasteful consumption. For more information visit www.panda.org

Kimberly Clark, founded in 1872, is an American multinational personal care corporation that produces mostly paper-based consumer products, like toilet-paper.

The Forest Stewardship Council (FSC) is an independent non-governmental organization, established in 1993 and dedicated to promote responsible management of the world's forests. The FSC sets standards on forests products as well as certifies and labels them as eco-friendly. The FSC logo means the materials used to make the product have been sourced from responsibly managed forests.

) How did the collaboration come about?

n 2003, Kimberly-Clark started requiring third-party fibre certification for ompanies in its supply chain. Three years later, it began developing a closer elationship with FSC. WWF entered into the equation shortly thereafter when Kimberly-Clark joined the organization's Global Forest & Trade Network, vhich works to improve the management of global production forests by ising the commitments, influence, and purchasing power of businesses to ring about market change. In parallel, Kimberly-Clark made time bound ublic commitments to source their paper from sustainable sources.

ast forward to 2011. Following many years of discussion and collaboration, Kimberly-Clark, WWF, and FSC launched the "Love Your Forests" ampaign, encouraging consumers to look for and choose FSC certified products. The "Love Your Forests" label links WWF's panda and the FSC ogo. Kimberly-Clark's leading brands Kleenex Cottonelle, Kleenex facial issues, and VIVA paper towel all featured the "Love Your Forests" label. These brands supported the campaign with consumer marketing and ocial media, including online, TV, in-store, and outdoor advertising. ?ropelled by the success of the "Love Your Forests" campaign, Kimberly-Clark launched a new three-year campaign in June 2017 called "Heart Your Planet." With this campaign, the company wanted to drive more awareness among consumers of the importance of choosing responsibly-ourced tissue products by looking for the FSC certification.

!) What were WWF's expectations for this collaboration?

Our expectations going into this collaboration were to work with ike-minded partners with the goal of promoting good and sustainable consumer choices as far as forest products, such as tissues, are concerned. Although this campaign took place in various countries, such as Germany, ve noticed a distinct opportunity for improvement in the Australian narket. During the development of this campaign in 2011, Australians used about 4 million tons of paper and cardboard, yet the awareness of ustainable forestry and forest products was under 10%. This number was astonishingly low and lagged behind other major markets, such as Europe and North America. To raise the awareness of the FSC label amongst the

Australian market, WWF and FSC needed the right partner: one with prominent brands, a large audience, a commitment to sustainable forest management close to its achievement, and a willingness to lead. That partner was Kimberly-Clark Australia. Our expectation going into this campaign was, together with Kimberly Clark and FSC, use the power of our brands, reach and scientific knowledge to shift trends for the better.

3) What did this partnership bring to Kimberly Clark and FSC?

According to Kimberly-Clark, the Love Your Forests campaign has helped differentiate their products in a crowded marketplace, and to communicate the company's environmental credentials.

> *"Through the Love Your Forests partnership, we've been able to use the strong reputation of our brands to raise recognition and understanding of FSC certification and responsible forestry with our consumers, and have pleasingly also seen a marked uptake in FSC certification right across the tissue sector."*

> Natalie Turner, Communications and Sustainability Manager, Kimberly-Clark

According to FSC Australia, prompted awareness of the FSC trademark among Australian consumers has more than doubled since 2011. With more and more consumers and businesses recognizing the importance of responsible forest management, and choosing products that carry the FSC logo, the future is looking brighter for the world's forests, as well as the wildlife and communities dependent on them.

4) What were the fruits of the collaboration and what did it finally bring to WWF?

In 2013, Kimberly-Clark Australia and New Zealand won three sustainability awards, including the FSC excellence award for supplier of the year, the Australian business award for environmental sustainability, and the Banksia award for leading in sustainability in large organizations. Kimberly Clark made huge progress in environmentally sourced paper and most of their products are FSC labelled. We had a whole communication process to emphasize the FSC label on the toilet paper. As the partnership was a success, consumers started asking for more environmentally sourced products. Therefore, other producers will start using FSC labelled products. And this virtuous circle is exactly what we wanted! The market offer is becoming more sustainable and once the awareness is high enough, WWF can move on to a new area of focus. Our strategy is to change industries and sectors by working with key players who are able to use their influence to bring others along. In parallel, Kimberly-Clark promised to invest funds to conserve the world's most precious forests.

5) Who worked on this collaboration?

This collaboration involved three parties: WWF, Kimberley Clark, and FSC. The consulting and communication teams came together to raise awareness of the FSC certification through the products' packaging and advertisements.

6) Overall, what were the best parts of the partnership?

The best part was when we saw the positive results of the survey! At the beginning of our Australian campaign, the FSC label awareness was at a very low level < 10%. We knew that the only way for more people to use the FSC labelled products was to increase its awareness. Thanks to the partnership, the awareness of the FSC label went from 5 to 15% in the first year and reached 25% after the third year! This is a huge win for us because increased awareness and demand for FSC product means an increase in the sustainable management and sourcing of forest products which is great for nature, businesses, and communities dependent on forest ecosystems.

7) What were the more difficult parts of the partnership?

Aiming to change consumer's habits through a short-term advertising campaign is challenging. So, we needed to come up with content and creative concepts that were really compelling and impactful.

On top of this, we had the complexity of developing and agreeing on a communication message with three parties involved; WWF, FSC, and Kimberly Clark. How to achieve all the objectives of all three parties in one go was challenging. But once we identified and defined our common goals and expectations, we were able to jump over these hurdles quite easily.

8) What do you believe were the keys to the success of this partnership?

For a partnership to be successful, it must be linked to both WWF and the partner's goals. In the case of marketing partnerships, our joint goals are to influence and promote sustainable behaviour or shine a light on a particular issue in order to drive the necessary change. In this case, all the three partners involved had a common goal, (increase the awareness and demand of FSC products and the equity of all brands involved) which allowed us to work in a collaborative and seamless manner. I believe having a common, long-term vision and being clear on each partners' expectations are key ingredients to successful bilateral or multilateral partnerships. In the end, we were able to increase the awareness of FSC, promote FSC certified Kimberly Clark brands, and promote sustainability throughout Kimberly Clark's entire supply chain. In the end, it was a win, win, win for everyone!

Also, I think the fact that we first started working with Kimberly Clark on transforming their business and supply chains really helped the campaign, as our content and creative was based on good science and results from the transformation partnership. Because of this, we knew each other very well as partners, since the collaboration started in 2007 and the marketing campaign came to life in 2013.

9) What parts of the partnership could have been improved?

The interesting aspect of this collaboration was that we could work in various markets which presented different opportunities and challenges. For example, in Australia, public awareness of forest issues and FSC was fairly low when we started the campaign, so this required a certain level of messaging and creative tactic. Conversely, Germany a high level of awareness. In hindsight, we should have adjusted our messaging to suit each market better, so we could make the right kind of impact per market. For instance, we could have gone beyond the FSC discussion in Germany, and touched on recycled paper and how to enhance its use.

0) What does WWF have planned for the future in terms of upcoming partnerships?

2022 is a big year for us, as this is our target date for our ambitious 2010 goal of doubling the numbers of tigers in the wild through the TX2 (tigers times two) initiative. On the corporate marketing partnership side, we are putting together a roadmap to help us figure out the most strategic and creative way to best engage brands which use the tiger either in its name, logo, or as design inspiration. Our vision is to create a movement of brands which will use their influence and reach to help us reach our TX2 goal through awareness and fundraising campaigns. You can find out more about the TX2 initiative here: http://tigers.panda.org/tx2/

REFERENCES

Austin, J.E. and Seitanidi, M.M. (2012). Collaborative value creation: A review of partnering between nonprofits and businesses: Part I. Value creation spectrum and collaboration stages. *Nonprofit and Voluntary Sector Quarterly*, 41(5), 726–758.

Cailleba, P. and Casteran, H. (2010). Do ethical values work? A quantitative study of the impact of fair trade coffee on consumer behavior. *Journal of Business Ethics*, 97(4), 613–624.

Dickinson, S. and Barker, A. (2007). Evaluations of branding alliances between non-profit and commercial brand partners: the transfer of affect. *International Journal of Nonprofit and Voluntary Sector Marketing*, 12(1), 75–89.

Lafferty, B.A. (2007). The relevance of fit in a cause–brand alliance when consumers evaluate corporate credibility. *Journal of Business Research*, 60(5), 447–453.

Lafferty, B.A. (2009). Selecting the right cause partners for the right reasons: The role of importance and fit in cause-brand alliances. *Psychology & Marketing*, 26(4), 359–382.

Lafferty, B.A. and Goldsmith, R.E. (2005). Cause–brand alliances: does the cause help the brand or does the brand help the cause? *Journal of Business Research*, 58(4), 423–429.

Lafferty, B.A., Goldsmith, R.E. and Hult, G.T.M. (2004). The impact of the alliance on the partners: A look at cause–brand alliances. *Psychology & Marketing, 21*(7), 509–531.

Larceneux, F., Benoit-Moreau, F. and Renaudin, V. (2012). Why might organic labels fail to influence consumer? *Journal of Consumer Policy*, 35, 85–104.

Sabri, O. (2018). The detrimental effect of cause-related marketing parodies. *Journal of Business Ethics, 151*(2), 517–537.

Sénéchal, S., Georges, L. and Pernin, J.L. (2014). Alliances between corporate and fair trade brands: Examining the antecedents of overall evaluation of the co-branded product. *Journal of Business Ethics, 124*(3), 365–381.

Torelli, C.J., Monga, A.B. and Kaikati, A.M. (2011). Doing poorly by doing good: Corporate social responsibility and brand concepts. *Journal of Consumer Research, 38*(5), 948–963.

CHAPTER 7

Brand collaborations with territories

Brand collaborations can also include partnerships with territories. These types of brand collaborations are more and more used, and focus on countries, cities, regions, and space. We can distinguish two kinds of brand collaborations with territories.

One practice consists of integrating the values of a territory within the brand identity in order to enrich the brand image. This practice is called the strategy of "the country of origin" (Lee, Lee and Lee, 2013). It is the case of Volvo (a Swedish brand car) referring to the culture of Sweden and using labels with the Swedish flag on its car seats. The goal of Volvo is to integrate Swedish values (safety, nature, large spaces, etc.) into its brand image, even if the cars are manufactured in China.

The second strategy is initiated by a territory looking for collaborations with brands connected to its culture or its place. In this case, highlighting brands from a region or a city leads to the promotion of the territory. For instance, the collective brand, "La Bretagne," groups 75 local brands and promotes knowledge of this specific region.

Table 7.1 Brand collaborations with territories

s of collaboration	Definitions	Examples
branded products tiated by brands	Collaboration with one brand and a territory involving a new product highlighting a territory's values (product line extension)	- Mini & Kensington - Asos & Kenya - Heineken & cities - Absolut vodka & cities
branded products ated by territories	Collaboration between a territory and one or more local brands involving the creation of new local products from the territory	- Comptoir Richard & Paris - Bretagne & 75 local partners

7.1 WHEN BRANDS LOOK FOR TERRITORY OF ORIGIN

To attract an increasingly demanding clientele, looking for significant experiences, brands collaborate with territories to offer bold and exclusive products. For instance, Asos put Kenya as a significant country on its website. Indeed, Asos launched a "Made in Kenya" collection with different partners: Soko Kenya, Kenyan supermodel, Leomie Anderson, and two Kenyan designers, 2ManySiblings. The mixed clothing collection, has a multitude of pieces, each more colourful than the other and promoting Kenya. The online retailer also worked with these different partners to improve the living conditions of the local community and to encourage sustainable development.

BHV, a French retailer, celebrated South Africa as a country at the heart of the international scene of design and fashion. The richness of South African culture, history, and art transformed the department store into a place of discovery and unprecedented experiences for consumers. To achieve this, BHV teamed up with the South African Tourist Office to offer the best destinations in South Africa to Parisian clients. BHV also partnered with Artlogic (an agency for galleries and artists) to select the best representative products of the country. In the end, the sales department brought together the biggest South African fashion and decoration brands revolutionizing African fashion. BHV offered a space of expression to youngsters, a generation driven by the desire to produce equitably.

Territories are also neighbourhoods that inspire the creation of products. For example, London's Shoreditch (a London neighbourhood) with its innovative, artistic, and casual ambiance inspired the creation of a model of the Mini – the Mini Shoreditch car. This territorial inspiration allowed the company to offer an over-equipped car model to a clientele attracted by the atmosphere of this particular London district. Similarly, the car manufacturer has launched two other models inspired by London neighbourhoods. The Mini Kensington, associated with the Royal Borough of Kensington and Chelsea, targets customers attached to its values and in search of exclusivity. The Mini Heddon Street, named after one of London's most legendary streets, combines elegance with the English lifestyle. These brand collaborations with names of streets or neighbourhoods show how territories express values and become inspirational in targeting a particular clientele.

Brand collaborations with territories (countries, regions, cities, and neighbourhoods) have become more frequent as they mean something to people who travel increasingly and remind them of distant cities and cultural stories.

The Absolut brand has also been inspired by cities to launch limited collections of its famous vodka bottle. Absolut Miami and Absolut Statehood are communications campaigns that have featured their home states (the 50 states of America and the District of Columbia) through the artistic work of 51 painters.

Image 7.1 *Mini & Heddon street*

Image 7.2 *Mini* & *Heddon street*

Heineken launched the global "cities of the world" campaign to encourage people to unveil the secrets of the cities they live in. With these collaborations Heineken looked for innovative ways to interact with their consumers and with citizens. In addition to the TV ad campaign, they provided online activities and a set of specially designed bottles to honour the cities of New York, Shanghai, Berlin, Amsterdam, London, and Rio de Janeiro.

The champagne brand of Veuve Cliquot provides a limited collection named after 29 cities, reminding the 29 countries of where the brand is sold. This kind of brand collaboration with territories is particularly successful when the feeling of patriotism for a country or a city or a region is high. These collaborations are based on the sense of belonging to a community and at the same time foster sentiment for a territory.

Within the strategies of brand collaboration with territories, "Made in" is a specific practice. Indeed, the "made in" claim highlights the country of origin. Each country has its own strengths and weaknesses in respect of

Image 7.3 *Heineken & cities*

its industries: Japan stands for an exceptionally high level of technology; China has a clear price advantage; Switzerland represents the guarantee of quality, reliability, and luxury; US products are perceived as very trendy and well marketed; Germany is well known for its engineering skills and cars; and France is the emblematic country for elegance and gastronomy. The use of "country of origin" for companies is very helpful for transferring the country's image to their own brand and for gaining an advantage inside one's own country when people express a preference for domestic products. Even if there are benefits for brands in making reference to their country of origin, there are two reasons to avoid brand partnerships with the country of origin (Feige and Annen):

1. When the brand is already strong and perceived as a brand from a country, it is not necessary for the company to communicate its country of origin. For instance, the brand Bosch (engineering and electronics) does not mention its German origin as this is already well known.

2. When the image of the country of origin and the desired image of the brand do not fit, it is recommended to avoid the mention of the country. For instance, it would be counterproductive to attach "Made in China" to a luxury brand.

In order to make a brand collaboration with a country successful, one has to ensure that the fit between the country image and the desired image of the brand is good. Be conscious that collaborations with a country of origin are not only useful for positioning and advertising in international markets – they can also be used for positioning purposes in the home market, depending on each country's preference for domestic products.

CONSUMER TESTIMONY

Emeline, 24-years-old, single, student, French, Starbucks & cities of the world (interviewed in October 2018)

Travelling was the only thing I wanted to do when I was young. I remember that when I graduated from high school, I searched for the university that proposed me the most trips and journeys abroad. I wanted to discover, learn new cultures, maybe see other ways of living. When I had the first opportunity to leave, I went to Rio de Janeiro. It was exactly as I expected – except I did not realize at first how lost I would be. I did not recognize anything, not in grocery stores or restaurants – sometimes even the food was so different! During the first week it was very hard and I needed the Internet so I went to Starbucks often. I purchased the mug with "Rio de Janeiro" written on it and every time I took a picture or communicated via Skype with my relatives in France, this mug was somewhere in the screen. It became an emblem of my localization. I had quickly the opportunity to move again and went, just to say a few, to the USA and Canada. It amazed me how easy it was to find a Starbucks and purchase a mug with "New

York" or "Montréal" written on it. As time went by, what was a kind of comforting joke at first became a habit. Everywhere I go, I need to buy my Starbucks mug with the name of the city. As Starbucks seems to be like everywhere, I always manage to get my treasure. Some people prefer buying some traditional stuff, but it doesn't fit with my tiny Parisian flat I have now, so I prefer having multiple mugs and making a wall with it! And every time I look at my collection it reminds me of London, Bombay, Kyoto, Sydney … so many memories!

7.2 WHEN TERRITORIES LOOK TO ATTRACT MORE PEOPLE

Nowadays, more and more cities develop their brand image to attract people, not just for the tourism sector but also to attract both companies and families to work and live there. The most famous cities which have created strong brands are Amsterdam, New York City and London. They have developed numerous licensing offerings giving a wide choice of products to promote their city (clothes, food, cosmetic, accessories, home decoration, etc.). They do not do much co-branding; in general, their products are signed only with the brand of the city without mentioning the manufacturer.

In an opposing way, Paris has built a strong brand, "Ville de Paris," which frequently makes use of the co-branding strategy. For instance, "Ville de Paris" launched a tea collection called "Parisian tea" with Mariage Frères (a tea brand) offering three package colours: blue, white, and red. Interestingly, this collaboration allows extending the brand "Ville de Paris" to Business to Consumer and to Business to Business clients. Ville de Paris collaborates with Comptoir Richard to sell individual chocolates designed with the symbols of the most famous Paris districts (Le Marais, Saint Germain des Prés, Montmartre, Champ de Mars) to restaurants and coffee shops.

Image 7.4 *Coffee Comptoir Richard & Paris districts*

Image 7.5 *Chocolate Comptoir Richard & Paris districts*

Image 7.6 *Tea Comptoir Richard & Montmartre*

Image 7.7 *Tea Comptoir Richard & Saint Germain*

Small cities use also brand collaborations to enrich their identity and improve their brand image. For instance, the city of Deauville collaborated with the brand Guy Degrenne (a French tableware brand), a brand from Deauville and a specialist in tableware, to make a unique collection of dishes. The goal of the seaside resort is to promote its brand "made in Deauville" in various tourist areas.

In another context, the two regions of Aquitaine and Midi-Pyrenees Region have created a common brand, South West France, to promote their agricultural sectors. These brand collaborations between two territorial brands aim to develop the agri-food sector economically. This new brand allows the promotion of the South West France territory worldwide, and especially in China. Today, this common name facilitates the networking of those involved. This partnership has built an entity that is more visible and more credible both nationally and internationally. With more than 250 official brands, the two regions pool their talents, their terroirs, and their stories.

When territories look for more visibility and search to promote their cultures, they may host a sport event – Rio hosted the Olympic Games in 2016 and Russia organized the Football World Cup in 2018. The academic literature about brand collaboration suggests that pairing an event with a destination will engender a transfer of image between the event and the destination. One survey (Xing and Chalip, 2006) demonstrates that the presence of any sport event increases the host city's activity ratings, but the event's activity ratings are higher only when the event is paired with a leisure city. An inconsistency between the activities of the brand and the territory negatively affect the evaluation of a leisure city. These findings suggest that the match-up between events and destinations is determined by the original image of the territory rather than by shared levels of a characteristic. Another study (Heslop et al., 2013) on the Beijing and Vancouver Olympics provides evidence that brand collaborations between places and the Olympic Games are not always successful in terms of positive carryovers for both partners. The familiarity of a country plays an important role in explaining the impact of country choice on the Olympic Games reputation. Moreover, the name format of the Olympic Games ("country name" Olympics) seems to be riskier when country images are strong and in opposition to core Olympic values (excellence, friendship, and respect). Indeed, the country dominates the nested concept of the brand that will emerge (Beijing Olympics). The other way around, the FIFA World Cup uses the less risky alternative name format of "FIFA World Cup *in* 'country name'." In this case, there is less potential for a negative reputational impact from a country whose image is not congruent with the event.

7.3 WHEN BRANDS CONQUER SPACE

Brands dream of space. Brands implement very creative campaigns in order to be associated with this unique territory. In 2011, Ardbeg Distillery (the producer of single malt whiskey), in cooperation with NanoRacks, became the first whiskey producer to consider the possibility of the distillation process in space, connecting consumers to the prestige of space-based research. NanoRacks sought and received permission from NASA for Ardbeg to undertake a company-sponsored research project to study what happens to a class of molecules called terpenes in the absence of gravity. Ardbeg wanted to find out if new flavours and tastes would be developed by whisky in oak barrels in the space environment, when gravity is absent. Ardbeg's partnership was made visible through worldwide publicity, from newspapers to social media, showing how its association with the International Space Station can advance its brand. From a scientific view, the data received from the Ardbeg space station programme could be a key component in developing future whiskies, foods, or anything where flavouring and tastes are critical. Ardbeg will now be able to see how protein crystals grow and gain insight into chemical structures.

Again within the spirit market, in 2015, Suntory (a Japanese brewing and distilling company) sent a number of their Japanese whiskies to the Nasa international Space Station to study the mellowing process in a different environment. Two groups of five whiskies were launched, one of which was on board the ISS for about 13 months, while the other was scheduled to remain there for two or more years. The spirits are being kept in the same conditions as they are on Earth, so the whisky makers can discover the effect that gravity has on the aging process. While the samples won't be available for sale, they will help pave the way for space-aged whiskies that you can buy (if they taste good, that is).

In response competition from L'Oréal Men's range, the Axe brand needed visibility in order to continue to maintain leadership in the deodorant market for men. The brand decided to invest approximately $3 million in organizing an international competition around its Apollo deodorant with the prize of a space trip. The commercial operation with Nasa was a huge success – it accounted for up to 20% of brand TO (€1.4bn brand) over the campaign period. In key markets (US, Brazil, and Mexico), Axe Apollo was the most successful launch of the last three years, tracking 13–17% higher (value sales) than the next biggest launch. The Axe brand became famous on a scale never seen before with 25 million YouTube views, 20 million visits to the NASA site and 22 winners in 23 countries who had the chance to get travel in space.

In the food market, brands have also been attracted by space – Pizza Hut has made connections with space since 2000. For example, the brand paid about $1.3 million to see its logo on the Proton rocket. In 2001, Pizza Hut became the first to deliver a pizza to the International

Space Station (ISS) after a year of collaboration between Pizza Hut and Russian nutritionists to adapt the recipe to the constraints of a space flight (15cm in diameter, vacuum packed in order to travel). The visibility of this collaboration presented an innovative image to Pizza Hut.

Finally, in the toy market, Lego understood the opportunity of being associated with space as one of enabling children to dream. The purpose of Lego is to inspire children to think creatively, and for that reason the brand collaborated with NASA in order to develop the next generation of space scientists and engineers. At the beginning of the collaboration, in November 2010, NASA put a small Lego shuttle toy onboard the Discovery shuttle and Lego used NASA branding on their space products. Lego created a special website with games, videos, and facts about space exploration. In 2013, 13 Lego sets were sent to the International Space Station and astronauts were filmed assembling the sets in weightless conditions. These videos were then downloaded for use in classrooms, where students could build the same models and then compare them with the Lego models assembled while floating in orbit. This unlikely partnership was a huge success, and the original three-year agreement has been extended indefinitely. The "Future of Flight" challenge was launched for older fans. The winners of this won a Lego trophy and NASA memorabilia, along with the opportunity to present their ideas to Lego and aeronautics specialists. It was a win-win collaboration for both brands. The Lego brand got to officially harness the excitement of the space programme in its products and NASA was able to conduct public outreach aimed at increasing participation in science and engineering.

TRANSCEND POTENTIAL MISCONCEPTIONS

Brand collaborations with territories of origin are not only useful for positioning in international markets, they can be relevant for positioning the brand in the home market.
Brand collaborations with territories enrich the consumer brand relationship, creating proximity and place attachment.

DS AUTOMOBILES

INTERVIEW WITH HUGUES FABRE
DS VP Brand Strategy and Experience – PSA group

"When a brand collaborates with a city"

Keywords: city collaboration, coherent story

Actors: DS, the Louvre museum

DS is the premium brand of Groupe PSA. DS has the ambition to embody French luxury know-how in the automotive industry. The original DS of 1955 was a clear statement of what French innovation and prestige meant. The name DS can be an abbreviation for "Different Spirit" or "Distinctive Series." Electrification is at the heart of product strategy as every new model launch starting with DS 7 Crossback offers an electrified version either PHEV (Plug-In-Hybrid) or BEV (Battery Electric Vehicle). From 2025 all new model launches will be electrified vehicles only (PHEV or BEV). DS Automobiles started participating in Formula-E in 2015, which is the world's championship for electric cars.

The Louvre, established in 1793, is the world's largest art museum and a historic monument in Paris, France. In 2017, the Louvre was the world's most visited art museum, receiving over 8.1 million visitors per year.

1) How do you choose your partnerships?

We have several aims for our partnerships, which could include reaching different audiences, getting in touch with opinion leaders, and displaying our core DS brand values and French-ness.

For DS, we have decided to break the rules of the status quo partnerships, and declared our brand ambassador not a celebrity, but a city. From 2015, Paris has been our brand ambassador! An international city, with millions of visitors a year, known worldwide for class, elegance, and history.

With DS, we've harnessed Paris's allure and claimed three classic Parisian symbols for our advertisements and included national French anthem *La Marseillaise* as the song of our advertisements. We are showcasing the Louvre, the Eiffel Tower, and the Louis Vuitton Foundation – three symbols that represent the avant-gardism and boldness that symbolizes Paris and complements DS's core values of French refinement, craftsmanship, innovation, and beauty. You will find these three images in all our communication tools worldwide.

Another daring partnership we did was becoming the first-ever car manufacturer to design a kitchen for famous French chef, Yannick Alleno, owner of several high-end restaurants in France and abroad, for his renowned Parisian restaurant *Pavillon Ledoyen*. The DS Design Studio actually designed the kitchen, and a DS logo was branded into the stoves. The chef drives one of our DS cars and is passionate about the brand. As you know, France is known for the refinement of its gourmet kitchen and excellence, which made this in line with our overall partnership strategy. We activated the partnership though strong storytelling in social media, behind the scenes footage, and PR. We invited our best clientele to dine in the famous restaurant *Pavillon Ledoyen* and meet the chef in a truly special visit.

Our partnership with Parisian fashion icon Ines de la Fressange, enhances our products through tactical limited-edition cars, including special premium features Ines endorses and designs together with us. In the short term, it's a way to increase the attractiveness of our range. We did these two partnerships with Ines in 2015 and 2017 – it could be interesting to see if this has long-term potential, as well as being a perfect fit for our brand!

2) What was DS's expectations for the collaboration with the Louvre?

Our sponsorship contract with the Louvre museum started in 2015. Like our brand DS, the Louvre combines history and futuristic modernity with its iconic pyramid designed by architect Pei. DS's partnership with Paris and its hree icons show the best of French design: iconic symbolism, boldness, and xcellence. We wanted to make our partnership with the Louvre something lurable and international, as it gives us a real opportunity to cement our rand and reach new audiences globally. Ideally, we are planning to activate ur partnership with the Louvre outside of France through its temporary xhibitions, which travel in all major museums worldwide.

) What did this partnership bring to the Louvre?

n our collaboration with the Louvre, we are both sponsors and partners. lence, our partner receives the perks of being both the giver and the eceiver. An exemplification of the latter was the 2016 exhibition of French rtist Bouchardon, which we sponsored. This brought financial support to he Louvre and, in exchange, we have the rights to images, VIP tickets, nvitations to events, and similar perks. Besides being financially supported hrough this event by DS, the Louvre, by hosting, gained even more notoriety nd press coverage worldwide, cementing its already secure place in history nd proving the heritage and prestige of its buildings and exhibitions.

) What were the fruits of the collaboration and what did it finally ring to DS?

n immediate global success for us was when our 2017 French elected 'resident Emmanuel Macron did his inauguration speech in front of The ouvre and drove the Champs Elysees in a DS 7 Crossback. The result was n immediate return on DS Automobiles awareness! This holds especially rue in China, as the Chinese are very fond of official presidential cars. Of ourse, we did not have a partnership with the French President!

nother result of our French excellence brand positioning was when car ental company Hertz choose our DS7 Crossback car to drive first class ir France customers from the plane's runway to the airport hall.

) Who worked on this collaboration with the Louvre in particular? And in eneral?

)ur communication team in Paris and the Louvre's global marketing team vorked together to find unique ideas corresponding to both the museum nd our brand.

In general, to secure and enforce our French luxury positioning, we invite all our employees to participate for several days at the DS Academy Camp. Through this academy, we are collaborating with the Van Cleef and Arpels School of the Richemont group, in order to initiate our employees into French luxury brands and French refinement, craftsmanship, and storytelling.

6) Overall, what were the best parts of the partnership?

DS and the Louvre share an ambition of excellence and balance between heritage and boldness, incarnated in particular by the famous Pyramid of the Louvre. These common values brought our teams together for a successful partnership. When we choose a partnership, the values of French excellence, entrepreneurship and boldness always need to be present. It's similar to a checklist, in which we look for these three to four key values in common – if our values line up with a potential partner's, we consider them for a collaboration!

7) And the more difficult parts of the partnership?

To keep fine balance of shared values. It is like a value mirror matching perfectly or even more: enhancing both partner images when together.

8) What do you believe were the keys to the success of this partnership?

In general, for a partnership to be successful, there need to be values in common. Along with mutual respect, no company should emerge solely dominant; it needs to be balanced in work, trust, and ROI. The best partnerships deals are win-wins! I also believe long-term partnerships to be the more successful. For example, our contract with the Louvre is four years long, and we will hopefully continue our partnerships with them after 2020! For a luxury car brand to become well-known and appreciated, it takes over a decade. Knowing this, we have to collaborate and fine-tune our partnerships and brand values of French luxury and excellence in the long run!

Another successful anchor of our partnerships is our Formula-E car races. It is a fascinating championship racing in the centre of all major global cities, including Paris, Hong Kong, New York, Berlin, and Dubai. It brings DS strong recognition and awareness, as well as a brand image of highly technical and innovative premium cars. It also support the development of our electric road cars thanks to our track to road approach. Remember: all of our car new car range is electrified.

9) What parts of the partnership could have been improved?

With the Louvre collaboration, I wish to improve the international aspect. It is a pity that we didn't yet managed to further expand our partnership with the Louvre abroad, as internalization is one of our strategic pillar, as well as one of the Louvre's.

Image 7.8 *DS & Michelin & Total*

Image 7.9 *DS & Givenchy*

REFERENCES

Heslop, L.A., Nadeau, J. and O'Reilly, N. (2010). China and the Olympics: views of insiders and outsiders. *International Marketing Review, 27*(4), 404–433.

Lee, J.K., Lee, B.K. and Lee, W.N. (2013). Country-of-origin fit's effect on consumer product evaluation in cross-border strategic brand alliance. *Journal of Business Research, 66*(3), 354–363.

Xing, X. and Chalip, L. (2006). Effects of hosting a sport event on destination brand: A test of co-branding and match-up models. *Sport Management Review, 9*(1), 49–78.

Conclusion to Part I

This first part has shown that brand collaborations can take many forms:

- with different partners (brands, artists, celebrities, cultural organizations, sports organizations, NGO, territories, etc.)
- with different outcomes (new products, co-communication, co-events, cross-sales promotion, co-distribution, etc.)
- and with different targets (consumers, employees, retailers, etc.).

These seven chapters have allowed us to have a complete view of brand collaboration and have shown how, nowadays, brands have numerous possibilities of forming partnerships with different actors and with different objectives. The main point of Part I has been to propose a new vision of brand collaborations that goes beyond co-branding. The analyses of multiple examples, and the testimonies of managers within international organizations, have introduced the idea that brands, looking to give meaning to employees, consumers, and citizens, need, on the one hand, to create and to communicate with partners and, on the other hand, brands need to show their partnerships. In this context of looking for meaning, we consider that brand collaborations include all associations between a brand and a partner as they are revealed to their targets (within or without the organization).

We are also in the era of co-creation, as companies look for brand appropriation. In this context, brand collaborations concern also consumer communities, regrouping individuals with a strong attachment for the brand[1] For instance, through its website "Nike by you" the brand launched

---

1 Cova, B. (2017). *La vie sociale des marques*. Edition EMS.

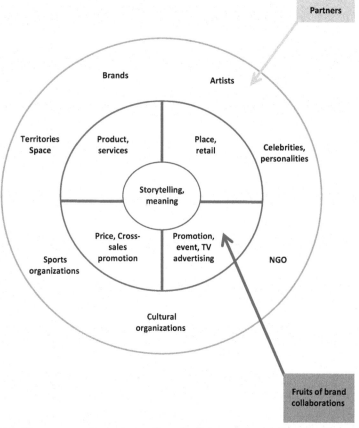

Figure 7.1 *The partners, the products of brand collaborations and the storytelling required to give meaning to multiple audiences (employees, consumers, partners, etc.)*

specific Air Max sneakers co-created with members of its fan community and supported by an ad campaign telling of this collaboration.

In conclusion to Part I, we can highlight the different strategies of brand collaborations in Figure 7.1.

We can highlight the main benefits of brand collaborations as follows:

The benefits of brand collaborations	*Examples*
1) Enlarging the brand target, creating more touchpoints	Vans & Van Gogh (Chapter 4)
	Johnnie Walker & Game of Thrones (Chapter 4)
	Lacoste & Roland Garros (Chapter 5)
2) Generating more visibility with important public relationship coverage	Louis XIII & Pharell Williams (Chapter 2)
	PSG & Nike & Jordan (Chapter 5)
	Disney & Chiara Ferragni (Chapter 3)
3) Launching innovative products	Evian & Kusmi Tea (Chapter 1)
	Airbnb & Lego (Chapter 7)
4) Creating brand experience	Pierre Hermé & L'Occitane (Chapter 1)
5) Enlarging the distribution network	Burger King & Pepsi (Chapter 1)
	McDonald's & Evian (Chapter 1)
6) Creating a premium image, differentiation	Iwatch Apple & Hermès (Chapter 1)
	H&M & Blancpain
7) Developing conversations in social media	Tommy Hilfiger & Gigi Hadid (Chapter 3)
	Nike & Kaepernick (Chapter 6)
8) Transforming the production system	H&M & WWF (Chapter 6)
	Coca-Cola & WWF (Chapter 6)
9) Motivating the internal work force, the company's internal creativity	Dior & MAD (Chapter 4)
	Bic & Yousef and Elias Anastas & Yann Santerre (Chapter 2)
10) Commitment to good causes	Volvic & Pilot (Chapter 6)
	Estée Lauder & Pink October (Chapter 6)

PART II

Key strategies and methods for successful brand collaborations

CHAPTER 8

Master the fundamentals of brand management tools

Before considering a brand collaboration, brand managers must know their own brand very well. Nowadays, brands are thought of as individuals and as social objects. To manage brands correctly you have to understand the importance of the brand identity, the brand's central core and the brand's legitimacy. Mastering these is one of the keys to a successful brand collaboration.

8.1 BRAND IDENTITY

Brand identity means the way the brand is defined and what it stands for, as opposed to its image, which is the way the brand is perceived by consumers. Brand identity is a guide for brand management. It guarantees consistency and continuity of the brand over time. It is why this tool is very important when defining a brand collaboration. The brand identity is helpful in deciding which kind of brand collaboration to put in place and for choosing the right partner. In the end, the identity of the brand operates as a guide for action. It serves as a framework for all decisions made by the company, on what the brand "should be and can do." The identity should be rich and meaningful but, above all, it should be expressed within the organization. The "brand platform" or the "brand book" are helpful tools. In order to define brand identity, we present here its four dimensions:

THE FOUR DIMENSIONS OF BRAND IDENTITY

The identity of a brand is a story that is organized around four attributes: ideology, personality, signs, and emblems. Seeing the identity of the brand as a story has the advantage of making sense and orchestrating the different attributes into a coherent whole (Berger-Remy, 2013).

1) Ideology: An ideology is a system of beliefs and values. The identity of the L'Oréal brand is based on the belief that the beauty of women is both sophisticated and cultural. This system of beliefs is opposed to that of Nivea, for whom women are naturally beautiful, the cosmetics products only revealing her to herself. This system of values is the basic element of the brand's identity story, it is that which gives meaning to the brand. In the context of brand alliances, the brand manager has to make the right decision about brand collaborations. The ideology of the Nivea brand allows it to collaborate with Special K (Kellogg's cereal brand), as they share the same values about beauty. Their complementary products for healthy food and skin lead women to be naturally beautiful inside and out.

2) Personality: Presenting the brand by making an analogy with the personality traits of the human being is an effective way of embodying it and thus fostering partnerships under its brand name. The richer and more imaginative the personality description is, the easier it is to find a relevant partner. For example, thinking of the Lacoste brand as a chic, sporty, authentic, and discreet person makes it easier to find a right partner. The Lacoste Roland Garros limited edition, in the fashion market, shows the good fit between Lacoste and the elegant Roland Garros, French Open Tennis Championship.

3) Signs: Signs represent the physical expression of the brand ideology and brand personality. It can be words (the name of the brand, the slogan) or forms (graphic, colors, textures, logo, character). The Bibendum mascot is the ideal representation of the generous, friendly, and helpful personality of the Michelin brand. The red cow of The Laughing Cow is the representation of the values of humour and playful childhood claimed by the brand. In the context of brand alliances, partners can play with their signs as in the Louis Vuitton collaboration with Jeff Koons. Or as, more recently, Lacoste

changed their logo when it collaborated with the IUCN NGO to save endangered animal species. And like the Jupiler brand (a Belgian beer) that changed its name to "Belgium" on their beer bottles during the five months of the World Cup.

4) Emblems: The emblem of a brand is the product or service that best conveys the ideology and values of the brand. It is elevated to the rank of symbol. It is not necessarily the best-selling product, but the one that, like Nivea's blue box, perfectly expresses the natural and basic values of the brand. In the same way, the polo shirt represents the successful mix of sport and chic for the Lacoste brand. In the context of brand collaborations, a company can team up with partners who revisit the iconic product. For example, Nivea and Bic produce co-branded products with different artists who bring new aspects, respectively, to the blue box and to the four coloured pen emblems.

n order to use brand identity correctly, it is important to understand the onnection between the four dimensions. The ideology, the personality, he signs, and the emblems are arranged in such a way as to constitute the ngredients of a coherent narrative. The ideology is the base of the story, t is the brand purpose. The personality represents the style of narration, t is the "style" and tone of the brand. Signs and emblems are the physical limensions of the identity that make the ideology tangible and illustrate ts personality (Figure 8.1). In the context of brand collaborations, the artnership between partners makes sense when it reflects and enriches he brand identity in all four dimensions. For instance, when Ikea ollaborates with Lego, or Adidas, or Olafur Eliason (an Icelandic-Danish rtist), it explores the boundaries of its knowledge and stretches the ossibilities of design. With Lego, Ikea explores design for the children hat are the adults of the future. With Adidas, Ikea explores exercise and ports within the home. And when Ikea partners with Olafur Eliason and is Little Sun Foundation it shows how it supports the sustainable project f bringing solar-powered energy to communities without electricity. These collaborations enrich Ikea's brand identity.

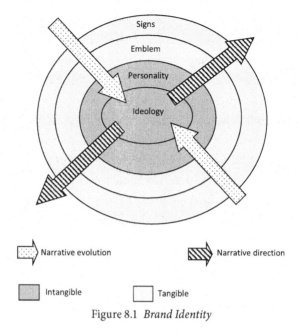

Figure 8.1 *Brand Identity*

THE MEANING OF THE BRAND

Brand identity is an important tool in brand management. However nowadays the identity of a brand is not built by managers on their own – several stakeholders contribute to the construction of brand identity. Consumers, especially, bring and add meaning to a brand because they make the brand their own. Lego is a good example, showing how consumers co-create the brand. Indeed, fans invent Lego constructions which demonstrate the values of "self-expression" and "playful learning" and some of them are selected by the company to be incorporated into the product range. These practices enrich the brand identity of Lego and lead to an amazing plasticity in the brand identity. Because stakeholders' brand appropriations drive brand identity, the brand manager's mission has changed. Brand managers have been often considered as "guardians," whose job is to control the brand through a set of rigid guidelines. Nowadays, the brand manager is more a "pilot" who must harmonize the various meanings contributed by stakeholders. And this vision is very important in managing brand collaborations that involve the ownership of the partner's values (whether for a long or a short time).

When the brand integrates the input of stakeholders, the brand identity evolves and becomes brand meaning (Michel, 2017). Applying the metaphor of a house, we can define brand identity as the house's architecture designed by the architect, and brand meaning as the life a house develops as a home. Just as a house does not exist without a foundation, a brand does not exist without an identity; and as home life does not exist without a house, the brand is not alive without the clients' ownership. Consequently, if stakeholders do not make the brand theirs, its identity stays stable. If some stakeholders try out and adopt the brand, they contribute to brand identity construction and generate brand meaning. In this case, the brand manager is no longer a "guardian," but a pilot. However, brand co-construction process is not possible for all brands. Not all brands have the capacity to collaborate with different partners in understanding their values and their universe. The art of brand collaboration lies in the capacity to find or to attract partners who can play with the brand identity and co-create brand meaning.

We have just demonstrated the importance of brand identity, and more particularly of brand values, to develop brand collaborations in the best way. In fact, for brand collaborations to be successful, they must be useful and give sense to consumers. Brand collaboration strategies are successful when they take into account brand meaning, because more and more clients appropriate the brand and enrich the brand content.

8.2 BRAND IMAGE

To set up a brand collaboration, the brand identity and brand meaning are not enough – we have to take into account the brand image, too. Consumer perceptions are essential in choosing the right partner and in defining the conditions of the collaboration. To understand the brand image, we now highlight the brand central core and the brand territory.

The image of a brand is a set of knowledge related to the brand. Brand image analysis is based on the identification and understanding of all the associations attributed to it by clients and non-clients. However, not all brand associations play the same role in the brand image. For instance, individuals used to associate "childhood" and "magic" with Disney. While "magic" is central to the meaning of Disney, "childhood" is a peripheral association, separable from the brand. Hence, to better define the collaboration between partners it is important to distinguish central and peripheral associations.

THE BRAND'S CENTRAL CORE

The central core is the fundamental element that represents the meaning of the brand for individuals. It integrates brand associations perceived by the majority of consumers as inseparable from the brand meaning. The core is the most stable element of the brand, the element that ensures its durability. The Nivea brand is, for example, perceived around three main central associations: skin care, natural, and accessible.

THE BRAND'S PERIPHERAL SYSTEM

Conversely, peripheral associations are strong but not inseparable from the brand. The peripheral system brings together strong associations, but they are not necessary to the essence of the brand. The peripheral system of the Nivea brand includes associations such as "men," "women," "child," "good smell," etc. These associations are separable from the brand meaning. It is possible, for example, for Nivea to launch a product which not dedicated to women.

Identification of the central core allows for a better understanding of the brand image in the consumer's mind. A brand collaboration is perceived as inconsistent when it does not respect the central brand associations. For instance, the collaboration between Nivea and pop singer Rihanna to celebrate the 100 years' anniversary of the brand was not a successful one –Rihanna's style and reputation did not match with the natural beauty (central core) claimed by Nivea. On the other hand, peripheral associations re not at the heart of the brand's meaning – it is possible for a brand collaboration to be inconsistent with the peripheral system (Michel and Donthu, 2014). For instance, even though the Hermès brand is not related to high tech devices, their collaboration with Apple in designing leather bracelets for iWatches was relevant and successful.

RECOMMENDATIONS: IDENTIFY THE BRAND'S CENTRAL CORE

First, you have to establish the brand's strong associations. Second, among these strong brand associations only some are central. In order to identify them you have to question the associations of the brand and to analyze the reaction of consumers to this questioning.

We can compare the central core of both brands to check if they match well or we can check to see if a partner fits well with the central core of a brand.

For example, the sports brands Adidas and Nike seem very close. Both brands are associated with the world of sports, streetwear and the greatest athletes in different sports. However, the perception of the two brands is different. The Adidas brand claims that sport is based on values of collective success ("Impossible is nothing") while Nike claims sport is the surpassing of oneself in an individualistic vision ("Just do it"). Indeed, Nike's vision is now "If you have a body you are an athlete," which pushes the consumer to excel. Adidas also pushes you to surpass yourself by suggesting to the consumer the idea that nothing is impossible for him. However, Adidas is more team-based than Nike – the new slogan "Adidas is all in" pushes for sports excellence by adhering to collective values (Figure 8.2).

The brand core helps identify its territory of credibility – this will guide the brand collaboration strategy.

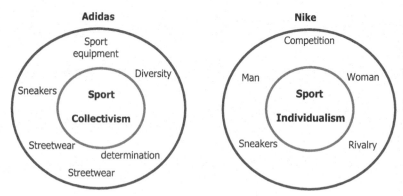

Figure 8.2 *The central cores of the Adidas and Nike brands*

BRAND TERRITORY

The brand territory corresponds to the territory where the brand is perceived as credible. Based on the central associations, individuals consider the brand more or less credible in investing new markets, in speaking or

Image 8.1 *Milka & Daim*   Image 8.2 *Milka & Oreo*

certain topics or in associating itself with a particular partner. The brand territory therefore integrates all areas of action and communication in which the brand remains consistent with its central associations. Thus, the territory of the brand Milka is defined around the pleasure of milky chocolate. This justifies it in making multiple brand collaborations, always in the world of the pleasure, with, for example, the brands Daim and Oreo in developing gourmet products.

Depending on the territory, brands have borders beyond which the development of products or changes in communications prove to be difficult. For instance, when the fashion designer Victor & Rolf designed a bottle for Piper Heidsieck (a French champagne brand), it was perceived by some clients as too extravagant – the central values of Piper Heidsieck were deemed to be more the transmission of a French, elegant style.

Brand image is a fundamental dimension in brand collaboration management because, beyond brand identity, it is essential to set up brand collaborations that take into account the perceptions of consumers. In a dynamic approach to branding, it is therefore crucial to identify the central core that defines the territory of the brand and this becomes a guide for the development of a brand collaboration.

8.3 BRAND LEGITIMACY

To carry out a brand collaboration it is also important to understand how brands build their legitimacy in the market. To build the legitimacy of a brand it is necessary to create meaning for the various stakeholders (Sinek, 2011). For that to happen, the brand must carry two messages: that of being (values and ideology) and that of doing (products and actions).

The brand holds values and an ideology (being) that it must communicate and prove. The brand must say who it is and must write its values and ideology into its products and communication actions. It is only when there is a balance between being and doing that the brand is perceived as legitimate by consumers (Zeitoun, 2016). Without legitimacy in its initial marketing, the brand collaboration may appear superficial. Before collaborating with a partner, the brand must have already demonstrated what it can achieve alone.

As part of a brand collaboration, therefore, it is essential to be aware of the level of legitimacy of the brand. The brand collaboration can then be part of the process of claiming its values. For instance, the DS car brand develops different collaborations with the French personality Ines de La Fressange (French model and designer), the Louvre Museum, the Louis Vuitton Foundation, and the Eiffel Tower, but always with the same goal. The DS brand wants to appropriate the magic of Paris, including its elegance, culture, and gastronomy. In its brand collaborations, DS shows a strong balance between its brand identity (being) and its products (doing).

In a brand collaboration, beyond an ephemeral partnership between two partners, brands must give meaning to people. For this, the brand's storytelling must differentiate two targets with different expectations (Figure 8.3).

1) The citizen is searching for meaning. He/she is waiting for a message that goes beyond the product. In order to meet these expectations, brands have to express the meaning of their collaborations. What do they want to claim?

Image 8.3 *Mini Cooper & Ines de la Fressange (French model and designer)*

2) The consumer is waiting for clear information about the product. From this perspective, the contribution of both brands must be clearly claimed. What is the added value of the two brands? Is the product useful?

To create legitimacy in a brand collaboration, therefore, it is necessary to inform the consumer of the brand's products and they must understand the inherent values in the brands. The cosmetic brand, Kiehl's, developed various brand collaborations, at the same time fulfilling the buyers' expectations of a good product and the citizens' desires to participate in a good cause (amFAR, the Foundation for AIDS Research). For example, as part of this collaboration, a limited-edition Ultimate Strength Hand Salve was developed. By purchasing this product consumers directly give to the good cause, while caring for their skin at the same time.

Giving meaning to people does not just mean collaborating with a good cause. The brand can give soul to products by referring to their values. For example, the collaboration between Evian and Spiderman (Marvel) gives meaning by highlighting the superhero's dream for children and Evian as a fount of youth.

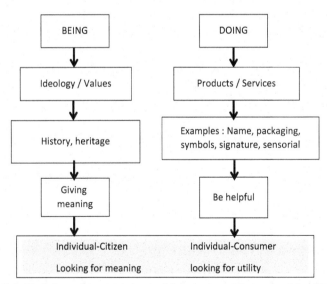

Figure 8.3 *The balance between being and doing, to meet the needs of the citizen and consumer*

Thinking through brand collaborations, balancing the meaning and the utility of the partnership, makes it possible to go beyond the storytelling and the brand content, as has been widely developed in recent years. This approach to brand collaboration considers the product, the experience and the values to all be at the same level of importance in fully meeting people's expectations.

REFERENCES

Batey, M. (2015). *Brand Meaning: Meaning, Myth and Mystique in Today's Brands* 2nd edition. Oxon: Routledge.

Berger-Remy, F. (2013). L'identité de la marque. In G. Michel (ed.) *Management Transversal de la Marque: Pour un Décloisonnement de la Marque dans les Entreprises.* Paris: Dunod.

Michel, G. (2017). From brand identity to polysemous brands: Commentary on performing identities: Processes of brand and stakeholder identity co-construction. *Journal of Business Research, 70*, 453–455

Michel, G. and Donthu, N. (2014). Why negative brand extension evaluations do not always negatively affect the brand: The role of central and peripheral brand associations. *Journal of Business Research, 12*, 2611–2619.

Sinek, S. (2011). *Start with Why: How Great Leaders Inspire Everyone to Take Action.* London: Penguin.

Zeitoun, V. (2016). *Nouvelle Perspective sur la Relation Marque-Consommateur La Mécanique Relationnelle Analysée à Travers le Prisme du Théâtre,* PhD dissertation, IAE Paris, Université Paris 1 Panthéon Sorbonne.

CHAPTER 9

Apply the traditional keys for successful brand collaborations

B rand collaborations involve creating something new that would not exist without the collaboration of both partners. The fruit of this partnership can be a product, a communication, an event, an exclusive distribution, etc. The goals of brand collaboration can be organised around five main objectives (Leuthesser, Kohli and Suri, 2003):

- to enlarge the target and rejuvenate the brand
- to extend the territory of the brand
- to tell a story regarding its values and draw attention
- to penetrate an international market
- to bring additional revenues.

To achieve the goals of brand collaboration, we highlight four main key strategies:

1) Brand collaboration involves a complementarity between partners.
2) Consistency in the product between the brand identity and the central core of both partners is important.
3) This consistency must not restrict surprising outcomes.
4) The fruit of any brand collaboration has to bring added value for consumers.

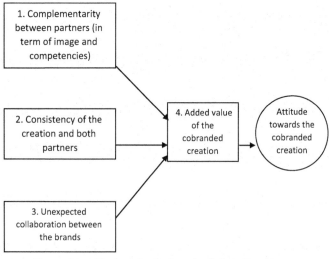

Figure 9.1 – *The keys for the brand collaborations success*

9.1 COMPLEMENTARITY BETWEEN PARTNERS

If brand collaborations are going to make it possible to better target an audience and capture more attention, it is necessary to ensure the perceived complementarity between the partners. Indeed, a brand collaboration that makes sense is one that combines values that will complement and enrich each other to ensure 1 + 1 > 2. Indeed, in the context of brand collaborations the proverb "birds of a feather flock together" is not appropriate. We would not go so far as to say that opposites are attract, but you must find an appropriate middle path and avoid marrying brands that are too similar. For instance, Uniqlo (a Japanese fashion brand) frequently collaborates with many artists who bring their creativity while Uniqlo provides the technology. Uniqlo is a textile laboratory while artists bring a style, a specific point of view that Uniqlo could not produce alone. Designers and fashion figures (such as Jil Sander, Jun Takahashi, Christophe Lemaire, Carine Roitfeld and J.W. Anderson) have enhanced the brand's aesthetic in order to bring a more fashionable pproach to Uniqlo's designs. These collaborations have put creativity at he heart of the Uniqlo brand, which a provides a wide range of clothes or all ages.

'o develop synergy, the partnership must rely on the complementary 1ature of the brands either in terms of image or in terms of knowledge. 'or example, the successful collaboration between BMW and the luxury •rand Louis Vuitton shows their complementarity in "The Art of Travel." 3MW, a car manufacturer, and Louis Vuitton are both in the business •f travel; they are known for high-quality craftsmanship in different ectors – cars and luggage. These shared values and the complementarity .re exactly why this brand collaboration creates brand identity for clients. n this partnership, BMW created a sports car model called the BMW 8, while Louis Vuitton designed an exclusive, four-piece set of suitcases .nd bags that fits perfectly onto the car's rear parcel shelf. The luggage ¿ts perfectly not only in terms of size, but its design and appearance fit •erfectly with BMW's image: sleek, masculine, and high-quality.

Image 9.1 *BMW & Louis Vuitton*

Image 9.2 *BMW* & *Louis Vuitton*

This collaboration between Louis Vuitton and BMW epitomizes the shared values of creativity, technological innovation, and style. In particular, this brand collaboration demonstrates the ingenious knowledge of Louis Vuitton and their attention to detail in creating a truly tailored set of luxury luggage. This is a pure expression of the central core of the Louis Vuitton brand "The Art of Travel."

These examples suggest that complementarity between partners is essential, especially to create value for consumers. If this is not the case, the co-branded product may be a failure. The failure of the sunglasses collaboration between Ray-Ban and Roland Garros can be explained by the fact that although the two brands were connected to the same universe of sport and prestige, there was no real co-creation and there was no added value for consumers.

Despite the importance of complementarity between partners, a survey reveals that similarity of brand personality could be an interesting factor in selecting the partner for a brand collaboration (Van der Lans, Van den Bergh and Dieleman, 2014). The survey, based on 1,200 brand collaborations, showed that consistency in brand personality profiles predicts a positive attitude towards a brand collaboration. More specifically, the authors found that similarity in character traits of sophistication and ruggedness and moderate dissimilarity in sincerity and competence result in favourable brand alliance evaluations. If we take an example from the Apple brand: it is because Apple stands out in excitement and sophistication, and because brand collaborations should be similar in terms of sophistication, that Apple is an especially attractive partner for sophisticated car brands such as Mini, Audi, Mercedes, BMW, Ferrari, and Porsche.

9.2 CONSISTENCY BETWEEN THE CO-BRANDED OPERATION AND ITS PARTNERS

Brand collaborations can be concluded with different kinds of partners and can generate different creations, such as a new product, a new advertising or a new event, etc. One of the most important success factors in a brand collaboration is the consistency of the co-branded creation with the brand identities of both partners.

When brand managers decide to collaborate with partners, they have to define the creation (product, event, communication, etc.) inspired by the brand identity and the central core of the brand. Putting brand identity at the heart of brand collaborations ensures the coherence and longevity of the brand. When San Pellegrino (an Italian water brand) associated itself with the jeweller, Bulgari, to create a limited-edition bottle, it was about having new stories to tell about the Italian culture of the brand. The co-branded product was therefore very consistent with the spirit of both brands and reflected the elegance and excellence of Italy, allowing it to position the co-branded product on the premium market.

The co-branded product must be consistent with both the brand identity and the brand image. From this perspective, the cooperation between

Adidas and Stella McCartney (a luxury clothing brand) is exemplary. The two brands have been associated since 2005 and each year offer a new line of chic sportswear clothing, consistent with the image of performance and style of the two partners. Adidas by Stella McCartney is a unique concept for women that features functional styles in running, gym, and swimwear.

RECOMMENDATION: TO MEASURE THE CONSISTENCY BETWEEN THE CO-BRANDED CREATION AND THE PARTNER BRANDS

Consumers can be asked three questions (on a seven-point scale where 1 = strongly disagree to 7 = strongly agree).

1) The co-branded sneakers fit with the idea I have of Adidas
2) The co-branded sneakers are perfectly in line with the idea I have of Adidas
3) The co-branded sneakers seem appropriate to the idea I have of Adidas

---

Complementarity and consistency are not always sufficient to ensure the success of brand collaborations; consumers are also looking for elements of surprise and the unexpected.

9.3 THE SURPRISING OUTCOME

The surprising outcome is also an important element in the success of brand collaborations (Fleck and Michel, 2012). The benefit of surprise is to bring the consumer into an in-depth cognitive process as the person seeks to understand why the two brands have collaborated. The effect of surprise is then beneficial as the consumer eventually comes to understand why the brands have joined together and becomes complicit with it (Fleck and

Image 9.3 *Lidl & Heidi Klum*

Quester, 2007). For example, the German grocery chain Lidl did not hesitate in creating a line of clothing with the German super model Heidi Klum. The aim was to develop the distributor's fashion department and it was also an effective communication lever for the opening of the first Lidl stores in the US. The "Heidi and the City" collection, inspired by her favourite city (New York), offers prices ranging from $6.99 to $29.99, and a real leather jacket at around $60. Thanks to this brand collaboration, the top model shows its proximity to women: "I wanted to create a fashionable and easy-to-wear fashion." Lidl enlarged its product range, demonstrated its role in the democratization of the fashion market and showed a more fashionable image.

Brands collaborating with partners from different universes raises the valuation of the partnership (Walchli, 2007). Indeed, brand collaborations can be innovative and surprise people. The marriage between the luxury pastry brand Pierre Hermé and the cosmetic brand L'Occitane demonstrates the success of an unexpected co-branding. The pastry chef opened the doors of his 1000m² concept store on the Champs-Elysées in

Paris, alongside the L'Occitane cosmetics brand. This collaboration shows the benefits of an unexpected marriage:

- This marriage between the worlds of gastronomy and cosmetics creates a new consumer experience – consumers discover exclusive products from both brands and assist in their manufacturing.
- The two brands offer are situated in an exclusive address and reach an audience in search of a "French-style" knowledge and experience. Indeed, the two brands bring an original emotional and sensory experience.
- This collaboration brings an important symbolic benefit and enriches the brand identities of both. Together the partners have created a new retail space and new products centred on French luxury. They also combine their own signs of authenticity: culinary versus natural, taste versus olfactory, artisanal versus patrimonial.

In the fashion sector the recent collaboration between the Japanese fashion brand Ambush and the American retailer Amazon shows the importance of surprise in raising awareness. Ambush unveiled its capsule collection in collaboration with Amazon on Instagram, showcasing a hoodie and

Image 9.4 *Perfume L'Occitane & Pierre Hermé*

a T-shirt with the caption "Work hard. Have fun. Make history." This collaboration was shown during the 2018 fashion week in Tokyo sponsored by Amazon. This unexpected brand collaboration gave more visibility to Ambush and permitted it to associate Amazon with the fashion universe through an inspiring message about a philosophy of life.

Still in the fashion industry, the unlikely collaboration between the American designer Heron Preston and the New York Cleanliness Service (DSNY) was a great success with the city audience. Clothing (t-shirts, caps, uniforms, etc.) based on the uniforms of New York garbage collectors and with the DSNY logo pay tribute to these shadowy workers. This collaboration within the department of Sanitation of New York makes visible the invisible. Most of the time, the spotlight is on firefighters and police and rarely on garbage collectors. The largest municipal cleanliness team in the world has been recognized thanks to this collaboration. This approach is all about the designer who has identified his brand identity and dreams of drawing the official uniforms of the staff of the DSNY: "It was my dream, at the beginning, to see the dustmen in the street, wearing the uniform of a designer." This unexpected marriage gives a sense to the consumers who participate in this tribute for people doing undervalued work.

A brand collaboration is a source of wealth that benefits from the fame of both brands. Some brands collaborate to blend two worlds and thus

Image 9.5 *Amazon & Ambush*

Image 9.6 *Amazon & Ambush Shirt*

expand their product range and reach a new target audience. Sometimes, in searching for originality, the partners lose the profit of the product. For example, the launch of the Milka and Philadelphia spread has not been very successful. The two brands, both from the Kraft Food Group, have combined their expertise in cheese and chocolate to offer a spread. However, while this product is very original, it does not satisfy the taste of consumers – it is too sweet or too acid – in 2012 the product stayed for only a year in the shelves of supermarkets.

9.4 ADDED VALUE FOR CONSUMERS

A brand collaboration should be considered only if it yields substantial benefits to consumers who are seeking product advantages in terms of utility and differentiation. When two brands join forces, the benefit to the customer should be greater than the offer from a single brand. For example, the combination of the Swedish brand H&M with the biggest names in fashion (Karl Lagerfeld, Balmain, Kenzo, Stella McCartney, and Moschino) allows them to develop clothing lines and accessories in the spirit of the great stylists at affordable prices. With these special collections, H&M is democratizing *haute couture* fashion, creating value for fashionistas. The added value, in terms of design and image differentiation, explains the success of the alliances between mobile phone brands and those of the luxury goods industry (LG & Prada, Samsung & Cerruti). In another context, the collaborations of Japanese brand, Hello Kitty, create added value because the co-branded products meet the expectations of Hello Kitty's fans. For instance, Puma's partnership with Hello Kitty meets the expectations of Hello Kitty fans who may not necessarily be passionate about Puma, but who dream of wearing shoes with the Hello Kitty style offered by Puma.

Many already well-known brands use brand collaboration to gain a competitive advantage, thanks to the exclusivity of the partnership. Indeed, offering its customers a unique offer that they are not able to find anywhere else remains an effective weapon against the competition. We have mentioned here only a few examples, and there are still many more (San Pellegrino, Italian water brand, and designers Missoni and Bulgari; the chain of Pottery Barn decoration stores in the United States and the famous paint manufacturer Benjamin Moore; the American retail chain Target and fashion designer Isaac Mizrahi, etc.), who have managed to offer really exclusive products.

RECOMMENDATION: TO EVALUATE THE
ADDED VALUE OF THE CO-BRANDED
CREATION

Consumers can be asked five questions (on a seven-point scale
where 1 = strongly disagree to 7 = strongly agree).

1) The co-branded product Puma-Hello Kitty is relevant in the
   sneakers market
2) Regarding existing sneakers, the co-branded product Puma-
   Hello Kitty meets the best to my expectations
3) Regarding existing sneakers, the co-branded product Puma-
   Hello Kitty is the offer the most interesting
4) Regarding existing sneakers, the co-branded product Puma-
   Hello Kitty brings something new
5) Regarding the others sneakers I know, the co-branded
   product Puma-Hello Kitty offers something better

9.5 ENRICH THE BRAND

Brand collaborations must certainly meet certain criteria to ensure
their success, but it must not be solely a question of the exploitation of
brand equity – it must also be integrated into the strategy of perpetuation
and enrichment of the brand. Before setting up a brand collaboration, two
essential questions to ask are:

- What does the co-branded creation bring to the parent brands in
  terms of image and customer experience?
- Do brand collaborations enrich the brand or is there a risk of brand
  dilution?

It may be hard to admit, but despite the success of a co-branded creation,
it is not always beneficial for the brand in the long run. When luxury
brands collaborate with lower quality brands, there may be a perception

of downscaling that may affect the luxury brand. For example, the luxury brand Kenzo collaborated with the French retailer Carrefour to offer clothing and linen lines. Despite the recognized quality of the products, the luxury brand was associated in the consumer's mind with the world of the mass market, the opposite world to the one claimed by the luxury fashion brand.

Sometimes a brand collaboration is not entered to increase sales but to feed the brand image (Cegarra and Michel, 2006). For its new advertising campaign, the e-retailer Zalando invited the German athlete Alexandra Wester, the French model Sonia Ben Ammar, the Belgian activist Hanne Gaby and the American singer Beth Ditto. These collaborations were not aimed at creating more sales. The choice of these four women celebrities and athletes showed the goal was to enrich the brand values of Zalando. The advertising shows us four talented individuals in their different environments, each wearing their favourite pieces of the new collection – for example, Beth Ditto appears backstage, as if she is ready to go on stage. The idea is to reinforce the unique character of women through these strong personalities who celebrate self-acceptance and appropriate their own style with the slogan "Fashion without limits."

To better understand the impact of brand collaborations on the partner brands, a study analyzed how arrangements and partner selections can influence evaluation of the brand and the recruitment of new clients (Newmeyer, Venkatesh and Chatterjee, 2014). Higher integration or longer durations of the partnership have a greater impact on evaluation of the brand and on the recruitment of new consumers. However, an exclusive collaboration has a greater effect on evaluation of the brand but lower recruitment of new clients than multiple collaborations. For instance, the collaboration between Häagen-Dazs and Baileys (an Irish Cream Whisky) met with great success from Häagen-Dazs' customers but it did not significantly increase the number of new customers. The existing customers appreciated this exclusive partnership between their favourite ice-cream brand and Baileys, allowing them to experience a unique flavour.

9.6 HOW TO AVOID BRAND COLLABORATION FAILURES

Although we have now identified the strategic levers, we must be cautious of collaborations that connect brands in different territories. This was the case with Milka, a famous brand of chocolate. In recent years, Milka has teamed up with various brands, such as Daim, Philadelphia, Lu, Oreo and Tuc, in launching new biscuits and new chocolate bars with new flavours. As a result, the brand image of Milka has become unclear, connecting the brand to "snacking" rather than to good quality chocolate. This example also highlights a main danger in brand collaborations: that of too many collaborations with too many different brands. Indeed, Mondelez, an American multinational company in the food industry, made the mistake of associating its different brands together and losing the individuality of the Milka brand. The multiplication of brand collaborations created too many products for consumers, who saw the Milka brand in every part of the store – biscuits, chocolate bars, and dairy products. The Milka brand has become more connected with the snack market and its image as good chocolate is gradually being diluted.

Brand collaborations can also generate a negative, green-washing image if the partnership with the good cause is not part of the brand's strategy. Partnerships and relationship strategies with non-profit organizations working to protect the environment can give a company an advantage over competitors, as it helps consumers believe that the products are legitimate. Partnerships with NGOs can provide the illusion of oversight from the non-profit organization, itself bringing legitimacy. However, this can appear to be just a strategy made up by companies to hide their damaging activities while improving their corporate reputation and brand image. It is important, for a brand to be perceived as sincere, to choose the right NGO partner. For instance, Heineken and Global Funds' partnership to Fight AIDS, Tuberculosis and Malaria received negative feedback as health actors claimed that alcohol is a major risk factor in he spread of HIV and tuberculosis. Consequently, this partnership was onsidered as inappropriate as it created a conflict of interest between the artners.

TRANSCEND POTENTIAL MISCONCEPTIONS

Avoid collaborations with partners who reflect too similar values because brand collaborations need complementarity to create added value to consumers.

It is not mandatory to choose brand partners who are leaders in their sector – the most important thing is the meaning of the collaboration. If you are creating a brand collaboration without meaning it is dangerous for your brand image.

Do not think that working with a small partner is not interesting – the most important thing is the collaboration. The partner with lower awareness can enrich a brand through bringing stronger values or a more premium image.

REFERENCES

Cegarra, J.J. and Michel, G. (2006). Les effets d'une opération de co-marquage sur l'image des marques. *Revue Française du Marketing, 207,* 61–72.

Fleck, N.D. and Quester, P. (2007). Birds of a feather flock together: Definition, role and measure of congruence: An application to sponsorship. *Psychology & Marketing, 24*(11), 975–1000.

Fleck N., Michel, G. and Gatignon, H. (2014). The dual process of co-branded new products: Why fit is not all that matters. Marketing & Innovation Symposium, Rotterdam.

Leuthesser, L., Kohli, C. and Suri, R. (2003). 2+2= 5? A framework for using co-branding to leverage a brand. *Journal of Brand Management, 11*(1), 35–47.

Newmeyer, C.E., Venkatesh, R. and Chatterjee, R. (2014). Cobranding arrangements and partner selection: A conceptual framework and managerial guidelines. *Journal of the Academy of Marketing Science*, *42*(2), 103–118.

Van der Lans, R., Van den Bergh, B. and Dieleman, E. (2014). Partner selection in brand alliances: An empirical investigation of the drivers of brand fit. *Marketing Science*, *33*(4), 551–566.

Walchli, S.B. (2007). The effects of between-partner congruity on consumer evaluation of co-branded products. *Psychology & Marketing*, *24*(11), 947–973.

CHAPTER 10

Discover new keys for successful brand collaborations

10.1 FROM PRODUCTS TO VALUES

Nowadays, brand management involves values because people expect more than just products. Brand collaborations have to be clearly defined in their goals so as to create brand identity for their target audience. Brands pay more and more attention to the consequences of their partnerships. For instance, FIFA's decision to hold the 2022 FIFA World Cup in Qatar is drawing more and more criticism – negative allegations about financial mismanagement and very poor work conditions are piling up. Some negative posts, featuring major sponsors that are continuing to support the World Cup 2022, are being shared on social media. Sponsors are sensitive to this issue and are asking for more transparency, while threatening to remove their sponsorship.

Because brands are more involved in society, they develop brand collaborations beyond their business. Google and Intel came together in an attempt to drive the IT industry towards greater efficiency with regards to consumer energy use. They added Microsoft, HP, and WWF to the mix and launched the Climate Savers Computing Initiative (CSCI) to get major companies to set targets and reduce emissions. Their cooperation has already resulted in a reduction of more than 60 million metric tonnes of CO_2. And, from 2012, the Climate Savers Computing Initiative has merged with the Green Grid consortium, with the same common goals: to improve IT resource efficiency and sustainability.

WWF collaborates with some partners who are not exemplary in social responsibility terms but the NGO also teams up with partners who need to improve their environmental impact. There is little sense in WWF collaborating with the eco-friendly fashion brand, Patagonia – what would be their environmental impact? The goal of WWF is to transform companies and improve their impact on the planet. In this collaboration, WWF stays independent and increase the positive impact of their partners on the earth. Beyond this transformational aim, WWF has created a product collection that has helped to highlight animal species and educate future generations. The slogan "take care of the planet" helps WWF make people feel concerned about the planet. WWF also works with employees of companies to raise awareness about environmental protection. For instance, WWF worked with Apple to develop "Apps for Earth," to make people more sensitive to environmental issues. All the revenues were redistributed to WWF. This kind of partnership shows that brand collaboration goes beyond the product and finds fulfilment in common goals.

When Nike chose the American football player Colin Kaepernick as an ambassador, Nike expressed a political commitment by partnering with a blacklisted, National Football League sportsman and criticizing Donald Trump for his action against the police brutality inflicted on black Americans. Nike is not afraid to recruit Colin Kaepernick, for their thirtieth anniversary of the slogan "Just do it." The brand claimed its values by launching an advertising campaign with the slogan "Believe in something, even if it means sacrificing everything." This slogan gains meaning when you realize that two years before this the athlete had knelt in protest against police violence against black Americans. The highly publicized scene created controversy within the National Football League, upset Donald Trump and Kaepernick's contract was not renewed at the end of the season. Nike publicly demonstrated its commitment to combatting police violence against Afro-Americans. This brand collaboration caused, on the one hand, discontent among some consumers who posted videos of them burning their Nike shoes; on the other hand, this campaign met with strong consumer support and contributed to a spectacular growth in Nike's sales.

10.2 FROM A WIN-WIN APPROACH TO SHARING THE SAME GOAL

With the development of innovative and original brand partnerships, companies are equipped with tools to quickly reach objectives that may seem difficult to access if they stay alone. Nowadays, the world moves fast and sharing of information is instantaneous and many-faceted. In order to keep up with the pace of development and to maintain their agility, brands need partners. Even if partnership does not always appear easy, collaborations place brands in more open strategic relationships and encourage them to explore common interests.

The partnership between the furniture brand IKEA and UNICEF (an NGO working to improve children's lives) shows that brand collaboration success comes when the partners work together for the same goal. Indeed, IKEA contacted UNICEF because of problems with child labour in its supply chain, and together they have improved the labour conditions of people working in factories in key locations, such as India.

In another context, WWF has developed brand collaborations only with partners whose mission is to create solutions that will solve the environmental challenges of the planet. WWF looks for partners in reaching their goal to save the planet as they are not able to achieve this alone. WWF works with companies to bring change through transformational partnerships. For example, WWF has collaborated with the Kimberly Clark company (a personal hygiene paper product company) on their forest footprint over many years. Only after significant improvement in their environmental impact has WWF decided to unveil this collaboration to the larger audience in Australia. Both partners have highlighted on the product's packaging the label FSC and they have developed co-branded communication about the preservation of forests. The goal was to increase the awareness of this label in Australia and to educate consumers about the responsible consumption.

This kind of partnership is developed with a long-term view to continue the improvement for several decades. For instance, the idea is that the partner supports UNICEF until the goal has been reached. Therefore, NGOs target founders or CEOs of companies to ensure that the partnership is enrolled in the company strategy and not just seen as a tactical operation. When partners work with a long-term perspective they are more likely to reach the common goal because they are both committed to the collaboration in terms of time and finance. The ultimate goal for NGOs is to stop working with companies – this will mean that NGOs will have accomplished their mission and that industries do not need their help in saving the earth any more. This is the dream for the future, when companies will be committed to social causes without needing NGOs to speak out and when social cause will be integrated into their own. For instance, the Unilever company does not need UNICEF to speak out and get their message across, because they already care very deeply.

10.3 FROM STORYTELLING TO STORY-DOING

Storytelling is the art of telling a story to serve the communication and brand awareness. Storytelling captures the audience's attention differently and, through the story it tells, the brand uses on emotion to entice customers (Woodside, Sood and Miller, 2008). When the brand Louis XIII collaborated with John Malkovich (actor and producer) and Pharrell Williams (singer) on a movie and a song about their product, the brand told a story about the 100 years of production of their cognac.

Story-doing goes further than just telling a story – it is the concrete participation of the brand in the life of society. When a brand supports a cause, in the long run, it embodies humanistic values. Story-doing makes it possible to confer a strong identity on the brand through long-term support. For example, Red Bull supports, many athletes and enables them to reach their sport challenges. Kiehl's has partnered with many celebrities (Julianne Moore, Brad Pitt, and Pharrell Williams) to support charitable causes (AIDS, Autism Speaks, etc.). These types of collaborations, with concrete actions, represent the future of brand collaborations because these actions are part of society and go far beyond the brand's products.

Today, consumers have high expectations of products. Puma understood it very well and is an active partner in culture, helping to move things forward and make the world a better place. The partnership between Puma and the actress Cara Delevingne for a campaign conveying the message "don't conform, don't worry about what people say," was a way for Puma to support Cara in her role as an ambassador of UNHCR (the UN Refugee Agency). All the personality partners of Puma and associations with NGOs are opportunities for Puma to support the good causes they promote. This mutual support helps both partners and, on top of this, makes the partnerships more authentic.

10.4 FROM CONSISTENCY TO FREEDOM OF EXPRESSION

In the fashion sector, the recent collaboration between the luxury brand Louis Vuitton and the skateboarding and clothing brand Supreme shows the importance of surprise in raising awareness and in creating value for consumers. The capsule collection Louis Vuitton and Supreme has developed contains clothes and bags inspired by the world of luxury and by street culture. We can explain this successful collaboration by its spirit of freedom – revisiting the Louis Vuitton monogram and inserting the colour red into the luxury articles. On the other hand, this collaboration has had other unexpected outcomes in respect of the relationship between the brands. The latest public announcement from the two brands was a lawsuit sent by Louis Vuitton to Supreme in 2000 for placing their famous monogram on skateboards. As a result, the American brand had to withdraw its collection from sale. Seventeen years later, things have changed again. Supreme has now become a worldwide phenomenon, a symbol of coolness and uniqueness, to which millions of fans have become devoted. This collaboration has shown Supreme as the streetwear brand whose products are the closest to those of a luxury home.

Image 10.1 *Louis Vuitton* & *Supreme*

Image 10.2 *Louis Vuitton* & *Supreme*

he collection is the perfect synthesis of the identities and heritage of oth brands: the irreproachable finishes and sleek design of the French, ne misappropriation and allusions to street culture of the Americans. he marriage of these two cultures, Louis Vuitton and Supreme, has reated timeless clothes that come with many accessories – the Louis 'uitton cap, bob and panniers, the "imitations" of street culture resented in official versions by both brands. We are here truly in a pace with freedom of expression. Louis Vuitton has often supported nnovation and street artists but this time it is officially at the same evel as a streetwear brand. This brand collaboration is a clever way f celebrating a global;y popular culture and, above all, to enhance s image with a younger and more perceptive audience. For its part, y partnering with the luxury giant, Supreme has demonstrated its trength – it is able reconcile the needs of both worldly hipsters and the nost demanding fashionistas.

n the sports market, the first collaboration between the soccer team PSG Paris Saint Germain) and the Jordan brand (Nike), their co-signing of ports items is more than an unexpected partnership, it changes the rules. he brand collaboration mixes, for the first time, the sources of inspiration f football and basketball. It comes with a series of almost a hundred roducts and is for a contractual period of three years. The success of this o-branding was immediate – supporters have rushed to the PSG website nd shops.

Image 10.3 *PSG & Nike Jordan*

Image 10.4 *PSG & Nike Jordan*

10.5 FROM SHORT TERM TO LONG TERM

The growth of limited-edition collections in the fashion sector has been seen as superficial, with only a business orientation and no specific meaning. Nowadays, individuals expect brands to show clear values and vision. Instead of always creating new products with different partners, some brands now maintain partnerships for long time. For instance, Uniqlo (the Japanese clothing brand) has continued its collaboration with Ines de La Fressange (the French designer) for five years, providing clothes with Parisian style within a philosophy of daily wear. Adidas has also continued its collaboration with Stella McCartney (a luxury designer brand) from 2005 to the present – the aim of this collaboration is to design a collection of high performance sportswear for women following the same code of ethics and the same modern ethos as the Stella McCartney collections. These enduring collaborations have created consumer brand relationships for the long term.

From a strategic point of view, the management of the brand today consists in creating strong brands – that is, developing brands that are well known to both employees and consumers (Michel 2017). To be totally in line with this perspective, it is important to think of brand collaboration in the long term – it's hard to share values and create brand identity with short-term brand collaborations. Although the Louis Vuitton and Supreme collaboration has been a major commercial success, their orchestration of co-branding around limited collections has limited the scope of this union between the world of luxury and that of "streetwear." Because the benefit of brand collaborations is to generate new phenomenon that could not be achieved otherwise, it is important to sustain brand collaborations over the longer term to anchor the brand in values and to create brand identity for consumers. For decades, the luxury fashion brand Repetto has collaborated with the Opéra Garnier in the design of slippers and outfits for dancers. The brand even chose Dorothée Gilbert (prima ballerina from the National Opera of Paris) as an ambassador for the luxury house. These brand collaborations, over the long term, have allowed the brand to enrich its sources of creation but, especially, to build its legitimacy in the world of classical dance and to be able to develop other products and fashion accessories around the world of ballet.

REFERENCES

Michel, G. (2017). *Au Coeur de la Marque, les Clés du Management de la Marque*, 3rd edition. Malakoff: Dunod.

Woodside, G., Sood, S. and Miller, K. (2008). When consumers and brands talk: Storytelling theory and research in psychology and marketing. *Psychology & Marketing, 215*(2), 97–145.

CHAPTER 11

The methodology for creating a brand collaboration

Now that you have learned in our previous chapters about what is possible in brand collaborations and the key strategies for successful brand collaborations, it is time now to move to the practical part and learn how to make it happen. In Figure 11.1, you will see the five steps of a brand collaboration project – from the beginning, when you get briefed by a brand wishing to do a brand collaboration or when you are the product manager of a brand that wishes to start a brand collaboration, to the fifth and final step when your co-branded product is finally on the shelf.

The five steps are all explained, one by one, in the following text. Together they represent the process of establishing a brand collaboration.

The time frame for bringing a brand collaboration to life varies. It can take several weeks for small, easy projects. However, it may take several years if it's a brand collaboration with many stakeholders – if, for instance, two or three major companies or brands are involved. In general, the average brand collaboration takes between one year and 18 months.

Again, the future is uncertain and even with your best endeavours you cannot always control negotiations of the contract (Step 4) if they become difficult, or if the artist's creative process takes longer than planned, or if the results do not meet the brand's expectations.

In the following sections, we provide concrete tools for overcoming the potential difficulties that can occur in a brand collaboration process.

We can distinguish five steps in developing a brand collaboration

1) Project framework
2) Strategic recommendation, screening and profiling

3) Contacts and project scope
4) Negotiation, closing a deal, and contract drafting
5) Project follow up and the creative process: until the collaboration comes alive!

11.1 PROJECT FRAMEWORK

This first section will cover defining your objectives clearly in orde to draft a project framework which you will use internally in you company. This framework will also help you to write a briefing in case you need to engage an agency or any third party helping you to find the partner with whom you wish to do your brand collaboration.

Always try to understand why you are looking to do a brand collaboration and why you are looking for a partner. Before going further in search o a partner, take time to draft an exhaustive framework to better define the approach and the key milestones of your brand collaboration: define your brand identity, your brand core, your main target, and why and how you would like to integrate your brand collaboration in your marketing strategy.

Last, but not least, don't forget that a brand collaboration can be one small part of the overall marketing strategy for your brand but it can also be the core, the main asset, that all of your other marketing activations are inspired by. You will find these two possibilities in the following figures. Some brands use a brand collaboration such as a limited edition capsule clothing collection as a method to activate their distribution channels or for PR purposes; others, like alcohol brands, may use a brand collaboration with a brand ambassador as a core part of their total brand and communication strategy.

1) *Executive Summary*: Indicate here the outline of the project: context scope, reasons why, overall objectives
2) *Defining your brand*:
   - Brand background (history, market share)
   - Market – Trends/situation/competitor analysis (competitive benchmark)

Figure 11.1 *The project framework should be composed of the following information*

- Brand developments and ambitions (strategy and vision for the brand: innovation, refreshing the brand, enlarge the target audience, etc.)
- Brand identity and positioning (brand positioning, brand promise, sales cycle, countries targeted, brand values, communication platform, strengths and weaknesses)
- Previous projects

3) *Defining your target audience*: Key insight, category relationship, consumer studies.

4) *Defining your brand collaboration project*:

- Project description
- Objectives of the brand collaboration
- Project scope
- Budget
- Constraints

5) *Defining your time frame*: Key deadlines of the project

In Table 11.1 you will find an extensive framework highlighting the different elements you should integrate into your project. Table 11.1 is based on the example of a brand wishing to do a brand collaboration for a limited-edition product.

Table 11.1 The project framework

1) *Executive summary*	*Examples*
Indicate here the outline of the project: context, scope, reasons why, overall objectives etc.	• The brand would like to identify an ideal partner for the realization of their limited-edition strategy • Within its cycle plan, the brand plans to launch one limited edition product, in line with its key activation periods of Summer (Holidays) and Winter (Christmas), in order to activate sales whilst building the brand image and creating appeal towards its key target audience, young females, 20–25 years • The brand is currently suffering from an old-fashioned image, and the limited-edition strategy should help the brand refresh its image and bring in a new relevance. It is part of the overall strategy of the brand to move from a functional image to a lifestyle/accessory brand • Previous attempts at co-branded limited editions without a signature approach with a famous personality have proven to be efficient in terms of sales but did not bring in the expected image boost. Therefore, the brand wishes to take the approach to a higher level

| Brand background
Indicate here your brand's background and current market position | • The brand is the historical leader of the market segment, and still benefits from a 30% market share on its key end markets Germany, France and Russia

• Launched in 1970 and famous for its creative input into classical cocktail dresses, the brand has built a strong leadership image over the years, and has reached a certain cult status

• With an awareness level of 93% it is positioned as the category leader, but unfortunately it has an increasing image deficit, as young brands with more transgressive and innovative approaches tend to attract the core target audience

• Innovations like a new range have helped to maintain the brand in its status, but lose impact in the long term. In 2019, the brand plans to launch its first limited edition capsule collection with a famous personality, introducing a completely new way of consumption to counterbalance and regain market share |
| Market trends/situation/ competitor analysis
Indicate here briefly the overall evolution of your category and your key competitors (direct/ indirect) | • After years of downturn, the fashion segment has seen an energetic comeback within our key markets over the last few years

• Over the years, the number of limited editions has increased within the segment, and now every brand brings out its yearly collection of limited-edition products. Standing out and making a difference has become much harder

• Direct competitors: Brand 1, Brand 2, Brand 3

• Indirect competitors: Private labels such as … |

(Continued)

2) Your brand	Examples
Brand development and ambitions Indicate here your plans for the future for the brand and the market position you are aiming at in general	• Overall objective: reaffirm leadership and stabilize the brand's market share at 30% by positioning the brand as a lifestyle brand embodying the target aspirations of fun and parties • Through an innovation pipeline based on three new limited edition launches in 2019 and an on-going limited-edition product approach for the years after
Brand identity and positioning Please add any presentation/ brand guidelines/communication material that you think could help us understand your brand	• Positioning: … • Unique selling proposition: … • Reason to believe (why can we say that): … • Brand values: … • Communication platform: … • Current weaknesses and strengths of the brand: …
Previous projects/activities for learning Please indicate here if you had any previous brand collaboration or similar activities as the ones planned, and what worked/what did not work and why.	The brand did not do any previous endorsement or brand collaboration, but only some limited-edition product activities that achieved only short-term sales increase without any image benefit (see execution examples attached)

3) Your target audience	Examples
Target audience description Please indicate here all the key data to know about your target audience: gender, age group, social situation, behaviour, etc.	Young, urban trendy females, 20–25, students or young actives. Low income, but highly fashion and lifestyle oriented/trendsetters
Key insights/category relationship Please indicate here anything relevant in the target audience's attitude towards the brand, the category, the consumption moment, etc.	What you wear is who you are, i.e. looking for the latest trends and always willing to stick to fashion. Following fashion influencers is part of the target audience's regular attitude Pay attention to what the target audience wears

4) The brand collaboration project	Examples
Project description Please indicate here shortly what type of brand collaboration you are looking for and for what usage.	Looking for a high level, international celebrity for leverage awareness and visibility through a 360° activation over a year Example Looking for a long terms brand collaboration with a celebrity as a spokesperson for the brand, embodying the brand values

(Continued)

4) *The brand collaboration project*	*Examples*
Objectives of the brand collaboration Please indicate here your business/ marketing and communication objectives for this specific operation	Business/marketing objectives: Develop a brand collaboration for two limited-edition products that help the brand to: • Leverage a long-lasting increase in market share • Drive additional sales • Generate trial among the brand's new target audience • Increases the number of loyal consumers • Gaining shelf visibility and leverage secondary placements within retail Communication objectives: Conceive the brand collaboration for two limited-edition products in a way that helps the brand to: • Generate public relationship and buzz and word of mouth without media support/ increase brand and product unit awareness at point of sales • Improve brand health and image indicators by rejuvenating the brand • Support or implement the brands new positioning among our existing target • Become relevant with the new, edgier target audience • Touch trendsetters • Help internal sell-in
Project and activation scope	All product ranges to be covered by the project: The whole brand, product ranges or one specific product/a new launch Footprint/key end markets to be covered by the project: France, Italy, Spain and China Exclusivity:

4) The brand collaboration project	*Examples*
Precisely how will you activate the brand collaboration	Instore and PR only, no budget for advertisings, etc.
	What do you want to do with this brand collaboration/which marketing assets?
	Above the line (ATL): TV, radio, cinema, print, online
	Below the line (BTL): point of sales, event, press
Indicate here what the ideal partner should and should not be, and how you would like to leverage him/her	Brand collaboration requirements
	What type of celebrity/partner do you have in mind?
	Actor, celebrity, fashion designer, musicians, brand, good cause, don't know yet
	What should he/she do for you?
	He should be able to design something, he should be able to provide content for a PR platform/content platform (concerts, making a film, a piece of art, a song…), he should convey above all the right message and be credible to do so, he's a famous face for my advertising
	What should he/she be?
	Trendy with the target audience, active on social networks, edgy, very famous in all my end markets, consensual, intellectual, strong political engagement, embodying a certain type of beauty/style, engaged with good causes, talks well in public, etc.
	International A-List star to leverage brand exposure, or a more niche artists to generate credibility, or maybe a local star to generate attachment
	What should he not be at all?
	Controversial, niche, too young, too old, too mainstream, to overexposed/already used by many other brands, political issues, drug and sex scandals, etc.

(Continued)

	Examples
4) The brand collaboration project	
Ideal world projection Are there any ideal partners you have already thought of?	You feel that the best fit for your brand is the USA rapper Kanye West … but you think you have not much chance to contract him, so you may think of other rappers in the same style …
Budget Indicate the budget you have for the brand collaboration	The Budget is a flat fee, with the possibility of including royalties on sales. NB: The budget does not include any additional money to activate the partnership, or limited edition, such as PR events, advertising, digital marketing activations etc. Another possibility is a win-win brand collaboration with no fee involved at all (nobody pays). This often happens if both partners put in similar efforts in terms of advertising, digital or promotions on either side of the brand collaboration project.
Constraints Indicate any other constraints to take into consideration	Local constraints, etc.

	Examples
5) Time frame	
Your key deadlines	• First feedback wished for DATE • Finalized concept and shortlist DATE • Internal approval/internal sell in DATE • Contract should be signed by DATE • Finalized brand collaboration for DATE • First creative inputs of the partner DATE • Production time constraints DATE

11.2 STRATEGIC RECOMMENDATION, SCREENING AND PROFILING

In this second step of the process of a brand collaboration we explore how to elaborate a recommendation and, once this defined, how to search for and identify your ideal partner. In the figure below you will see why certain brands put limited edition products on the market as a cobranding strategy, and what benefit their brands obtains.

BENCHMARK AND IDENTIFICATION OF THE IDEAL PARTNER PROFILE

Before launching your brand into a brand collaboration, it is important to know if your competitors do any brand collaborations. If yes, what type of partners do they collaborate with and how do they activate and communicate around their brand collaborations? Is it a long-term strategy or only a one-off? Do all their markets participate, in one global brand collaboration, or is it mainly local? It can also be very beneficial to investigate more general market trends – how do collaborations evolve in

Table 11.2 The selection criteria

Heighten brand recall and awareness		*Generate value transfer to shape brand identity*
Build brand status and image		Endorse your product through a relevant celebrity
Create an emotional attachment		Attract new audiences
Make the brand message stand out (PR, etc.)		Win in-store

Image 11.1 *Senseo*

other countries or continents? What are the trends in Asia, China, and the United Sates? What are the trends in marketing activation? Are the common communication tools digital or print advertising or something else? All of this information will help shape your knowledge and skills in elaborating a collaboration strategy which is outstanding, different and with a better ROI than your competitors.

Last, but not least, by establishing your benchmark you can also get a feel for the budgets your competitors pay for particular celebrities and others with whom they partner. For example, in the cosmetics industry, well-known actresses are used to endorse advertising campaigns for perfumes and they are typically paid very well. In order to make a significant difference, and if you don't have a large enough budget, you could collaborate with a less well-known singer or actress or you could restrict the collaboration to a digital endorsement only.

KEY POINTS FOR BRAND COLLABORATION BENCHMARKING AND YOUR STRATEGIC RECOMMENDATION

- Analysis of the direct and indirect competitive environment – what type of brand collaboration, what field (fashion, street art, sports)
- Overall market trends in brand collaboration. What are the best practices?
- How does your competition activate? What are the general activation tools employed?
- Conclusion: in order to stand out, what field, what type of brand collaboration would you envisage? What is your recommendation to stand out, to elaborate a successful brand collaboration?

n your strategic recommendation, you must follow your findings and he conclusions of your benchmarking and advise which type of brand ollaboration your brand should follow – in what field, what type of artners, and how to activate the partner in order to stand out:

- Field (music, art, sports), theme (trendy, flowery, premium)
- Pre-selection of potential partners
- Activation ideas – first approaches

STABLISH YOUR LONG- AND SHORT-LIST OF 'OTENTIAL PARTNERS

his part of searching for the right partner is always a very interesting ection of the brand collaboration process. You will need to dive eep into the Internet to find names, artists, brands, to double check nformation, to read newspapers, to view specialised Internet sites on a articular subject, and much more. For example, you'll have to become specialist in fashion in order to find the next hip clothing brand your ompany wishes to partner up with; or dive into space if your brand is ooking to endorse astronauts; or go to concerts of rappers if your brand nvisages doing a brand collaboration for young adults, etc.

ometimes managers know exactly what they are looking for and sometimes hey hesitate between several fields, between fashion and sports, for instance. n this case, you should make a list of potential partners per theme.

Develop a complete list of potential partners according to your chosen hemes. Your list should be fully screened against

- Feasibility considerations (budget, territories, awareness)
- Competitive problems (exclusivity, for example, if the potential partner had already been involved in partnerships with your competition)
- Brand fit evaluation

'ou should end your listings with your ideal partner – for instance, a top hree.

s an example, you will find in the Tables 11.3, 11.4 and 11.5 several election criteria which a brand defined in order to find its ideal partner.

The criteria are defined by: age/profession/skills/nationality/location previous brand collaborations/video on or with him/news/languages exhibitions/awards/social media coverage/designs, visuals or images of hi art/brand fit/others.

You can present your ideal partners in PowerPoint slides – one slide pe potential partner describing and showing in pictures his art if it is an artist what are his upcoming events, his background, links to his digital networks a YouTube video on which you can see him talk to evaluate if he speaks wel in public, if he speaks English, other languages important to your marke etc. and most importantly showing the fit between the partner and you brand. Table 11.6 takes the artist Vincent Van Gogh as an example.

Table 11.3 The selection criteria

1) Initial selection criteria: storytelling
• relevancy to brand and target audience
• Strong visual identity
• Recognized in their field
2) Secondary selection criteria: practical aspects
• Location: gain time and money in short negotiation timings + transportation costs
• Language skills: mandatory
• English speaker
• Multimedia artist:
• able to design a product
• Pre-existing social
• media followers to build a campaign on
3) No-go areas
• Recent partnerships with the brand's competitors
• Scandals, bad
• behaviour, drug and
• alcohol issues
• Too close to
• competitors'
• territories

Table 11.4 In an ideal world

Profile	Male, 25–57 years old, presents well, speaks English
Location	Time difference +/-5 hours from Paris
Skills	Painting and video arts (artist has own design studio, DJ skills)
Style	Kinetic/op art/digital art – funky, young. Relevant target audience and strong visual identity
Recognition	Relevant exhibitions in main galleries/ museums, strong social media followership, pre-existing strong partnerships
Other	Not a street artist No drug/alcohol issues No previous partnership with competition

Table 11.5 Detailed screening preselection

	Artist 1 40 years' old, video artist and experimental filmmaker	Artist 2 n/a years' old, kinetic artist	Artist 3 34 years' old, multidisciplinary artist	Artist 4 31 years' old, street artist
ile	+++	+++	+++	+++
ation	---	---	-	+++
ls	+	-	++	++
e	+++	+++	+++	+
ognition	Exhibition +	Ex + partner +	Partner +	Social media +
er	+	+	-	+

Table 11.6 Vincent Van Gogh, Painter 1853–1890, Dutch

Activities and key facts:	Brand fit
One of the leading figures of the post-impressionist movement, Van Gogh's paintings have marked generations of art lovers and are a part of the collective memory. he's certainly one of the world's most famous painters and immediately recognizable previous partnerships:	Optimistic*** Open-minded**** Encouraging** Unapologetic**

- 2018 Vans
- 2018 Samsonite

Why him/her:
His iconic imagery such as Starry Night, and his use of pointillism create an immediate recognition and are well-loved items used by brands for iconic limited editions. His work is a part of popular culture.

Image 11.2 *Van Gogh's painting*

THE MOST IMPORTANT ADVICE

If none of the potential partners you contacted are willing to do a collaboration with your brand, try to understand why – maybe it is a budget problem and they wish to get paid more; maybe your brand does not fit with the premium image of the partner; maybe they have had many other partnerships and are not willing to do any others at the moment; maybe they are in an exclusive deal with one of your competitors; maybe they do not have any affinity with you; maybe they are against tying their image to a brand selling alcohol, cigarettes, or cars. Once you know the exact reason, you can adapt your project and search for other partners. In general, it is always good to have a list of backup names. When you do your first research, always keep aside names of potential partners who are not necessarily your first choice but who could eventually fit if the other ames are not willing. You can also broaden your backup list by enlarging ne theme – maybe your search for fashion partners could be enlarged by dding fashion bloggers, and well-dressed actresses.

1.3 CONTACTS AND PROJECT SCOPE

Once you have decided upon your wish list, the exciting part of contacting and maybe meeting your potential partner – i.e. a famous nger, football player, designer of a hip hop clothing brand or a video rtist – comes to life! Below you will find two types of emails, or telephone/ n-person conversations, that you can have to establish a first contact with n artist, or any other type of partner.

CONTACTS

Most contacts can be found on the Internet. Often, famous personalities n music, cinema, and sports have agents who represent them. Often nese agents, who have a portfolio of personalities they represent, are rouped into major companies like IMG, WME, and others. They all take percentage of the deal they will negotiate on behalf of the celebrity they epresent (between 10 and 20% or more).

n other cases, you can find the contacts easily on their websites or social etworks, etc. In general, the more direct contact you have with the otential partner the better, as the information you get is less diluted and hus more accurate.

efore contacting your potential partner, make sure you have done your omework by having all the necessary information to hand. Make sure ou know all about their latest news, upcoming events, breakdowns, ormer collaborations, political issues, etc.

Double check that there is no conflict of interest – that the famous fashion esigner hasn't, for example, sold his fashion brand to a holding which ontains other brands in competition with your brand. Last, it is always wiser to contact your Top Five/Top Ten list of potential partners to maximize the chances of closing a deal rapidly.

FIRST CONTACT EMAIL

Send a first contact email without mentioning your brand name. It is more secure not to mention your brand in the first contact email, but only your market – for example, a luxury north American cosmetic brand. This secures confidential information and an initial natural selection can happen. For example, some partners are already engaged in an exclusive brand collaboration in your brand's market segment. Others are not willing to collaborate with anyone or don't have time for additional projects.

SAMPLE FIRST CONTACT EMAIL

Dear Mr, Mrs XXX

I work for one of the most premium electronic lifestyle brands and we are contacting you with regards to a worldwide brand collaboration opportunity.

Indeed, in order to promote one of our products, we would like to collaborate with you to participate in the realization of an exclusive line of unique products, packaging, and an art masterpiece that will be used mainly for communications purposes. We discovered your original creations and feel that you could be the ideal potential partner for this brand collaboration project.

If you have an interest in the proposition above, we will be more than happy to send you all detailed information about our company, our brand, and the overall detailed brand collaboration opportunity.

Many thanks in advance for your kind reply, and please feel free to contact us for any queries you may have.

Best regards

SECOND CONTACT EMAIL

Once you've received a positive reply to this first email, saying that they are interested to know more about the brand collaboration project, you can send the second contact email found below, containing the brand name and the project scope. The project scope details the overall project, including the fee, the communication details, the duration of the project, territory, etc. At a later stage the project scope is used to draft the contract. If you wish to keep the information (project scope) confidential, as you target different artists/personalities, you may require the partner to sign an NDA (Non-Disclosure Agreement) in advance. Also, always remember to mention that your brand is still in the selection process, especially when you are contacting several potential partners at the same time.

SAMPLE SECOND CONTACT EMAIL

Dear XX,

Thank you very much for sending us back the signed NDA.

Please find below more information about our brand and the brand collaboration project.

Our brand is XXX, a very well-known and premium electronic consumer lifestyle brand.

Please find attached a presentation and herewith a link to the website, where you will find more information about the brand, its markets and positioning

We would like to know if, keeping in mind the information hereunder ("Summary of the project"), you would like to consider our brand collaboration proposal.

If yes, we would be very pleased to set a date for a conference call or a meeting together with you and or your team to discuss this great opportunity in further detail and see what is feasible and eventually refine the scope and the timings below.

Last but not least, please keep in mind that this project is strictly confidential and that we are still in a selection process.

Looking forward to your feedback, I remain available for any questions that you may have.

Best regards,

PROJECT SCOPE

The project scope details the overall project of the brand collaboration, including the fee, the communication details, the duration of the project, territory etc. At a later stage, the project scope is used to draft the contract.

EXAMPLE OF A PROJECT SCOPE

SUMMARY OF THE PROJECT

The brand wishes to develop, with the participation of the artist, a limited edition (LE) of its products to be released in September 2018.

THE BRAND AND THE ARTIST: WORK AND INVOLVEMENT

Hereunder is described the work and involvement that will be provided by the brand and by the artist during the cobranding:

1. Design

The brand will provide a precise design brief for the limited-edition products to the artist, including all constraints of production colours, deadlines etc.
- The artist will create several designs to be used on the brand products and packaging.

- The brand and the artist will exchange on the designs
- If necessary, the designs can be adjusted by the brand's design agency. All designs need to be transferable to all ATL, BTL and online materials.

2. Distribution channels

Hypermarkets, supermarkets, e-shops, specialized stores, online stores, mail order houses, traditional electronic retailers

3. Marketing and communication

Above the line (ATL) – advertising to a mass consumer through broad platforms
- TV campaign
- TV sponsoring/billboard with the limited edition (+ name and logo of the artist)
- TV tag with the limited edition (+ name and logo of the artist)
- Billboards
- Print
- Radio

Below the line (BTL) – advertising on a one-to-one basis with specific consumers

Digital activation

- Announcement and communications of the collaboration on the brand's digital platforms and the artist's digital platforms
- Publication of videos on social media (Facebook, Twitter, Instagram etc.)
- Digital campaign around the limited edition launched on targeted websites
- CRM (emails and newsletters sent to B2C clients/prospects of the brand and B2B distributors)

Press and public relations

- Public Relationship events with the presence of the artist
- Press release/Press kit/Press conference/Advertorial
- Pre-launch of the limited edition at high-end stores: 1 Launch event, 10 interviews with the artist, 1 making-of / inspirational video with the artist, 1 hour availability for Q&A on the brand X twitter or another digital platform: the artist will discuss about this co-branding with Internet users
- Public Relationship gift: 100 limited editions items signed by the artist, 1 specific edition designed and signed by the artist and sold at auction for a good cause the artist supports

Point of sales

- Windows & in-store displays (wobblers, banners, key visuals, product demos, any other materials.)
- Brochures, distributors' catalogues
- Special customer promotions with the design of the limited edition: making-of video on TV screen in-store, pop-up stores

Internal

- Key visuals with the limited edition used for internal presentations (iPad, PowerPoint, etc.)

4. The partner (artist, brand, institutions, etc.) image rights

The artist name, photo and logo to appear on:

- Products and packaging
- In-store promotional materials (banners, posters, key visuals and any other POS materials)
- Digital platforms as well as those of third parties the brand X chooses to work with across owned, earned and paid media, including third party content creation - in press materials/ print advertising

- Media coverage in relation to this cobranding
- Events
- Samples
- All distribution channels of the brand X: all shops, wholesalers and/or retailers, corners, and through mail order selling, and/or by online selling and social networks.

5. Duration:

From July 2017 (first contact) to July 2019 (end of stocks)

Launch of the LEP by September 2018

6. Territories: Worldwide
7. Budget: Flat fee of €XXK not including any royalties on sales
8. Exclusivity/Non-compete

The artist cannot collaborate with any other electronic consumer lifestyle brand for the years 2018 and 2019

9. Provisional schedule

August 2017: Design brief from the brand to the artist + contract negotiations

End of September 2017: First designs sent to the brand by the artist + signature of the contract

October–November 2017: Back and forth between the brand and the artist

December 2017–January 2018: Product design validation

January 2018: Launch cobranding PR plan

March 2018: Packaging validation

March–April 2018: Final designs selected and applied on artworks (samples + cups)

September 2018: LEP in store

THE MOST IMPORTANT ADVICE

Often you send the project scope out at an early stage of the project and you're not always sure about the bigger picture your brand collaboration project will involve. It is always wise to see the bigger picture at an earlier stage, incorporating all potential needs in terms of communication tools, events etc.; at a later stage, you can downsize it to what you really need. Indeed, having to add amendments to your contracts and negotiating additional advertisings, per events, and creations generates additional costs. In general, the better your brand knows what it wishes to do and what the project entails, the easier it is to negotiate the brand collaboration deal.

11.4 NEGOTIATION, CLOSING A DEAL, AND CONTRACT DRAFTING

In this section, we will look at the art of negotiating, how to close a deal, and the best way to draft a contract.

NEGOTIATION

As we learned in the previous three sections, you draw up and send the detailed project scope, detailing the ins and outs of the potential partnership to your potential partner. In an ideal world, it would be great to get an official acceptance by return email saying they agree with the proposal. You can then start drafting the contract using the project scope. The drafting of the contract is either done by the legal department of your company or by an independent lawyer specialised in licencing and property rights.

Often the points the potential partner wishes to negotiate are on the financial side – they might wish to increase the fee they will be paid for

1e brand collaboration, or whether they will get paid if the project is
elayed. Other potential sources of friction can come from exclusivity,
y not wanting to being stopped from signing another similar deal with
1e of your competitors and the duration of such an exclusivity clause.
ometimes an artist may think they will have to give too much creative
1put and might wish to limit it. On the communication side, some
ersonalities do not wish to do any advertising, or to sign with their name,
s it will give them too much exposure – this might not be in line with
1other project they are working on. Sometimes the number of interviews
1d travel expenses needs to be re-discussed.

1 general, there are always solutions, and a middle way is often found
 conclude the agreement. But bear in mind that the contract should
lways reflect a win-win situation, where both parties are happy with the
ollaboration to come!

Vhen you are negotiating a brand collaboration contract, always make
1re that the person who signs on behalf of your potential partner (actor,
ports celebrity) is the official representative. Ask to have the official
greement of this representation annexed to your contract. Sometimes
1e fee that you are paying your partner needs to be paid in full to the
gent, and you need to make sure that the money arrives in the right
ands.

CONTRACT STRUCTURE

1 Figure 11.2 you will find the elements (i.e. articles) you should find in
our contract. It is more advantageous to have the contract signed *before*
ou start your collaboration, i.e. before the artist starts designing his first
leas for your brand collaboration. In the real world, however, contracts
re often only finally signed way after the creative work has started and the
rst meetings have taken place.

Article 1 Meaning of terms

Article 2 Object

Article 3 Creation of the limited-edition product

Article 4 Marketing actions

    4.1 Creation of the marketing materials

    4.2 Public relations (PR) events, internal events and interviews

    4.3 Advertising campaign

    4.4 Digital

    4.5 POS materials

Article 5 Intellectual property

    5.1 Use of the trademarks and the artist's property

    5.1.1 Use of the trademark

    5.1.2 Use of the trademark of the brand

    5.1.3 Use of the artist's property

    5.2 Intellectual property of the work product, design A, design B, and the artwork

Article 6 Term

Article 7 Termination

Article 8 Territory

Article 9 Exclusivity

Article 10 Compensation

Article 11 Approval process

Article 12 Warranties and indemnifications

Article 13 Relationship of the parties

Article 14 Assignment/sub-license

Article 15 Notices

Article 16 Miscellaneous

Article 17 Confidentiality

Article 18 Applicable law – jurisdiction

Appendix 1 Limited-edition product timetable

Figure 11.2   An example of a brand collaboration agreement between a brand and the partner, agreeing to collaborate together on a limited-edition product

THE MOST IMPORTANT ADVICE

During the contract negotiation you will have a lot of back and forth, and you will see many amended versions of your initial contract. Make sure that all parties amending the contract are mentioned separately and that you can clearly see their comments. Before signing the contract, always have a final proof reading to make sure everything is correct. While rare, it is possible to find phrases or amounts added that you were not aware of. Often in the case of non-respect of the partners' contractual engagements – e.g. timelines not respected, creations not sufficient, political issues, drugs or sex scandals of your partner – the contract foresees in its articles the fact that your brand can step out of the deal and, to a certain extent, be refunded. Keep in mind that you can always, and at any moment, decide not to pursue a deal, which can also be a negotiation tactic. Sometimes you need to amend the contract as your company wishes to extend the duration, or the project scope has changed and you wish to re-brief the artist.

11.5 PROJECT FOLLOW UP AND THE CREATIVE PROCESS: UNTIL THE COLLABORATION COMES ALIVE!

Now that you have found the ideal partner for your collaboration, and you have managed to succeed in closing the deal and signing the contract, it is now time to start the creative process. Certainly, you have already had several meetings with your partner and you have briefed them on the brand collaboration work that you are expecting.

THE CREATIVE PROCESS

In certain brand collaboration scenarios, where you wish for artist to make a limited edition product for your brand, you will need to clearly brief them on what you wish to see in terms of deliverables, what is possible or not, creatively speaking, and what timelines you foresee.

For some other brand collaborations, you only need the physical appearance of the celebrity, or their presence on a photo shoot or at an event. Whatever you require from your partner, always communicate clearly and largely in advance.

The aim in this part of the process is to maintain a smooth running, optimally organized relationship throughout the duration of the brand collaboration. You have several efficient tools at your disposal – such as sending out an agenda before a meeting starts, writing down and sharing a short recap of the creative meeting you just had with all stakeholders, so that in the next meeting everybody is on the same page and knows what is expected and respects the deadlines.

SAMPLE AGENDA

Date, Friday, 22 June, 1:00 pm – 4:00 pm

Location (address and directions)

Participants (name and contact)

> Brand 1/ Creative Director/ Category Manager/ Sales and Development Manager/ Talent/ Agent and/or Manager/ Agency Side/ Account Director

Keys points and objectives of the meeting: timing, next steps

> Introduction and presentation of each participant
>
> Presentation of leads, designs, creative intentions
>
> Finalization of products
>
> Next steps and provisional planning
>
> Schedule

PRODUCTION

Once the creative process is done, production time begins. Sometimes the production entails the making of a co-branded capsule collection or a photo shoot for a co-branded advertising campaign. All in all, remember that all co-branded materials need to have the official approval of your partner before you can put them on the market. Make sure you have written acceptance efore releasing anything. If you need to produce an event or interviews with ιe press for the launching of your brand collaboration, make sure you have :hearsed a speech with your partner beforehand in order to make sure your artner says what is expected of them and has all the information necessary efore going into the media arena.

nage 11.3 *Philips Senseo coffee machine limited edition with Japanese artist Sasu*

"HE MOST IMPORTANT ADVICE

'arious issues may occur at this stage: it could be that the creative routes ιre not feasible due to technical constraints which were not foreseen in your ιitial briefing; or the creative outputs are not appreciated by your brand. ι this latter case you might need to adjust your production timings, and r pay your partner or someone else (a creative design agency, perhaps))r the additional work. Before resolving the issues contractually, you an always find diplomatic ways to resolve the problem although it might :quire much more effort.

Conclusion to Part II

Chapters 9 and 10 highlighted the classic and new keys to succeed a brand collaboration. In particular these two chapters allow going beyond the classic rules of brand collaborations. You know now that the most important thing, for a successful brand collaboration, is the meaning and the added value brought to employees and to consumers. To create value, the both partners have to think their partnership as an opportunity to overpass their products and their short-term objectives in order to create new experiences inside of companies and in the market.

Chapter 11 has explained and given you all tools necessary to effectively bring a brand collaboration to life. You will now be able to correctly complete the following steps:

PLAN A BRAND COLLABORATION

Plan your brand collaboration by starting to write down a framework by listing your objectives, the constraints of your brand, and the reason behind the wished brand collaboration.

Explain how to achieve an ideal output for your brand and the brand's audience: what, how, with whom, when & where. Don't forget to incorporate in your framework:

- Trend watching
- Competitive benchmarks
- Consumer research

- Brand collaboration communication platforms & concepts,
- Partner profiles,
- Touch points & activation planning.

FIND THE PERFECT MATCH

Who you wish to ideally work with. You will master the art of "matchmaking" from profile screening to a finalized contract, all to be negotiated on your terms

- Partner identification & screening
- Project management in respect of given timelines (contacting, follow up, …)
- Deal Negotiation
- Legal expertise for contract elaboration and follow up.

MAKE THE BRAND COLLABORATION WORK

How to maintain a smooth running, optimally organized relationship throughout the duration of the brand collaboration from your first contact with an artist/personality to agenda management with the artist's agent to the organization of the overall project to the shooting of an advertisement to mediation with your partner internally to resolve a conflict.

Conclusion

A partnership can be considered an act based on the principle of the exchange of economic value between at least two entities. And, as in any transaction, the agreement is possible only if the value exchanged feels equal for both partners. However, this book shows that brand collaborations are rarely just an exchange of economic value. It is all about sharing, co-creation, innovation, and commitment between partners, who nourish their symbolic capital and generate economic benefits. From this perspective, this book has shown that brand collaborations can be concluded with multiple partners, take various forms (a new product, a new communication axis, an exchange of access to distribution modes, new communities of customers, etc.) and meet very different brand objectives. These include:

1) Enlarging the brand's target, more touchpoints
2) Generating more visibility with important, public relations coverage
3) Launching innovative products
4) Creating brand experience
5) Enlarging the distribution network
6) Giving a premium image and differentiation
7) Developing conversations on social media
8) Transforming the production system
9) Motivating the internal workforce and the company's internal creativity
10) Committing to good causes.

In the end, the story the brands tell enables a synergy with their customers, building strong relationships, which become a major benefit for the brand collaborators. As shown in examples throughout this book, brand collaborations can be as valuable for small and medium-sized companies as for the biggest, global brands.

In addition, our book has shown that brand collaborations are successful and benefit both partners if they respect a certain number of criteria (complementarity, added value, surprise, consistency), and if they exceed certain received ideas. Brand collaborations are not just short-term, one-off partnerships to create limited editions of products. Brand collaborations represent an important strategy which can be used to rejuvenate brands and keep them up-to-date. As presented in this book, brands can collaborate with partners to proclaim values and to become more committed within society.

Today, brands are no longer just signs to identify and differentiate products – they claim values and brand identity. From this perspective, collaborations bring new life to brands by using customized partnerships. Brand collaborations become a source of inspiration for innovation, and a resource to enrich the symbolism of brands. This reflection leads us to enlarge our vision of brand collaborations, and questions the place of brands in society.

In this perspective, we highlight the cases of Kering and LVMH (both French luxury groups) who have signed a joint partnership to redefine the working relationships of top models and celebrities, which will be applied to all of their brands around the world. They communicated together about this partnership, showing that both groups place respect for the dignity of women and men at the heart of their values. The CEOs of both Kering and LVMH agree that they want to be a source of inspiration and to bring real changes to fashion models' working conditions. This example illustrates the idea that brand collaboration can also be a strategy to exercise power in the market. The impact of this collaboration, their common voice, is more powerful than the same action by just one brand. The same idea lies behind H&M's collaboration with WWF concerning water sustainability, and their common call to change the textile industry's bad habits of polluting water. Together, brands can enact real change within a system.

A new era of brand activism has arisen. This is exemplified in recent campaigns: Levi's "Use Your Vote" campaign encouraged Americans to participate in politics during election season; Nike partnered with football player Colin Kaepernick to support the Black Lives Matter movement and stand against racism; Nike also endorsed tennis champion, Serena Williams, to highlight sexism and encourage and inspire women through sport. Through the activism of these brand collaborations (and many more!), we are witnessing a true shift in modern day business.

Finally, the topic of brand collaboration is not only a managerial issue, but also a social phenomenon that shows how signs, symbols, and brands are sources of inspiration for creating – showing the zeitgeist – and that the associations between brands and multiple partners are increasing. The future will definitely hold more collaborations between brands and good causes, enhancing social issues, pushing brands to show their activism and what they stand for. At the same time, innovation will be an important tool, offering even better products and services through well-thought out and tailor-made partnerships.

All in all, brand collaboration is about telling good, compelling stories with authenticity and sincerity that will be heard, spread, and thus successful.

We can't wait to hear your story!